Au

How to Keep a
Spiritual Journal

How to Keep a
Spiritual Journal

A Guide to Journal Keeping
for Inner Growth and Personal Discovery

RON KLUG

Augsburg
MINNEAPOLIS

To all the friends who shared with me the story of their journals

HOW TO KEEP A SPIRITUAL JOURNAL, Revised Edition
A Guide to Journal Keeping for Inner Growth and Personal Discovery

Large-quantity purchases or custom editions of this book are available at a discount from the publisher. For more information, contact the sales department at Augsburg Fortress, Publishers, 1-800-328-4648, or write to: Sales Director, Augsburg Fortress, Publishers, P.O. Box 1209, Minneapolis, MN 55440-1209.

Publication history: Thomas Nelson edition published September 1982; Bantam books edition published March 1989; first Augsburg Books edition published 1993.

Scripture passages, unless otherwise noted, are from the Holy Bible, New International Version, copyright © 1973, 1978, 1984 International Bible Society. Used by permission of Zondervan Publishing House. All rights reserved.

Scripture passages marked NRSV are from the New Revised Standard Version of the Bible, copyright © 1946, 1952, 1971, 1989 by the Division of Christian Education of the National Council of the Churches of Christ in the USA. Used by permission.

Scripture passages marked TEV are from the Good News Bible—Old Testament: copyright © 1976 American Bible Society; New Testament: copyright © 1966, 1971, 1976 by the American Bible Society. Used by permission.

Scripture passages marked PHILLIPS are from J. B. Phillips: *The New Testament in Modern English*, Revised Edition, © 1958 J. B. Phillips. Used by permission of the Macmillan Company, New York.

Cover and book design by Michelle L. N. Cook; cover art from Stock Illustration Source

ISBN 0-8066-4357-9

The paper used in this publication meets the minimum requirements of American National Standard for Information Sciences—Permanence of Paper for Printed Library Materials, ANSI Z329.48-1984. ♾ ™

Manufactured in the U.S.A.   AF 9-4357

06   05   04   03   02   1   2   3   4   5   6   7   8   9   10

Contents

Chapter 1

Why Keep
a Spiritual Journal?

A journal or diary (the terms are used inter-changeably) is a daybook—a place to record daily happenings. But it is far more than that. A journal is also a tool for self-discovery, an aid to concentration, a mirror for the soul, a place to generate and capture ideas, a safety valve for the emotions, a training ground for the writer, and a good friend and confidant. This book will show you how to begin a journal and how to use it for spiritual growth.

But what is spiritual growth, and how does it take place? This chapter explores these basic questions and the role of spiritual disciplines, including journal keeping.

Why keep a journal? Chapter 2 outlines the benefits as I have come to know them from my own forty years of journal keeping and from many friends and students who have shared their journal-keeping experiences with me.

How do you get started? What kind of notebook should you use? When should you write, and how much? Chapter 3 takes up these basic questions.

What goes into a journal? Chapter 4 outlines the type of entries you might make and gives you some questions to guide your daily writing.

Once you're started, how do you establish the habit of journal keeping and use it for your spiritual growth? Chapter 5 suggests specific actions that will keep you moving in the right direction.

Chapter 6 will introduce you to some additional journaling tools like unsent letters, altered perspectives, and lists to help you go further in understanding yourself and dealing with personal problems.

In chapter 7, you will learn ways to use the journal to care for your soul, writing exercises you can use in connection with spiritual reading and prayer.

To understand yourself in the now, it is helpful to look at where you have been. Chapter 8 will give you a number of ways to explore your own journey and even to begin sharing your life story with others.

Chapter 9 shows you ways to gain new vision and energy for your future, set goals, and move forward.

Do you catch yourself saying, "I just don't have enough time?" Chapter 10 provides some journal exercises to help you make the most of your time.

New research establishes the fact that journal writing is a way to receive healing. In chapter 11, you will explore areas in which you have been wounded in life and discover diverse ways to use a journal to cope with depression, deal with grief, overcome addictions, and open the way to personal wholeness.

How can you keep your journal private? How can you find time to write when you're already busy? Will a journal reinforce your problems by making you too introspective? Chapter 12 discusses these problems and shows you how to avoid or overcome them.

What do you do with the journal after you've written it? Chapter 13 suggests a number of ways to harvest the journal, to learn from it, share it, and extend its benefits.

The Guide for Forming a Journal Group outlines ways to form a support group to discuss the book and begin or enrich the habit of journaling.

From my own journal writing and from teaching journaling to people of different ages and backgrounds, I am convinced that a journal can be a major tool for spiritual growth. But before we turn to that topic, let's look more closely at just what a journal is.

The Spiritual Journal

I like this definition:

> A journal is a book in which you keep a personal record of events in your life, of your different relationships, of your response to things, of your feelings about things—of your search to find out who you are and what the meaning of your life might be. It is a book in which you carry out the greatest of life's adventures—the discovery of yourself.[1]

A teacher of journal writing, Metta Winter, summarizes:

> The personal journal is a private space of quiet and solitude: a place to befriend yourself and to explore the uniqueness of your life's journey. For centuries men and women have written in journals in times of loneliness, crisis, transition, conflict, spiritual quest, physical or intellectual challenge, or serendipitous joy. In these journals they have found companionship, emotional release, clarification, resolution, the self-affirmation required for courage, the discovery of spiritual resources, and a deeper appreciation of their lives.[2]

A journal can be used for many things: to record history, to keep track of the weather or the movement of animals, to outline one's work, to gather raw materials for writing and speaking. But in this book we will look at journal keeping at its deepest level—for *spiritual growth*.

Growing in Grace

Spiritual growth does not refer to some aspect of life or one compartment labeled "religion." It concerns all of life—our goals, our time, our relationships, our work, our politics, our inner lives.

We grow spiritually as we become more and more the people God wants us to be, and that means more and more like Christ. In the ongoing process of conversion, the image of God is restored in us. Paul wrote, "And we, who with unveiled faces all reflect the Lord's glory, are being transformed into his likeness with ever-increasing glory, which comes from the Lord, who is the Spirit" (2 Cor. 3:18). In that process our selfishness is transformed into caring, our rebellion into obedience, and our despair into hope.

"Grow in the grace and knowledge of our Lord and Savior Jesus Christ" (2 Pet. 3:18). When we hear this word from God, we may receive it as bad news, as a threat or demand. But properly understood, the command to "grow in grace" is good news, because what God wants for us is best, and what God commands he also empowers us to perform. God is eager to give us the means whereby to grow.

God places us in the church, in relationship with other believers. Here we are fed by the word and nourished by the sacraments. We grow as we worship God together with other believers, as we pray, meditate, tithe, and practice simple living. God brings people into our lives—people we need and who need us. From them we receive encouragement, comfort, and challenge.

Most important of all, God places the Holy Spirit within us to transform us, to shape our lives, to empower us, to make us more loving.

All this God does out of grace, undeserved goodness. The path to spiritual growth is a path of grace.

If the Christian path is one of grace, what is the place of self-discipline in spiritual growth? Our disciplines—things like fasting, prayer, contemplation, and journaling—are a response to grace, not an alternative to it. They are a way of being open before God, of giving the Spirit a chance to work in us.

Donald Bloesch, in *The Crisis of Piety*, pinpoints the proper function of spiritual disciplines:

> These disciplines must not be regarded as meritorious; rather they should be seen as having practical value. They strengthen us in faith and ongoing sanctification. They are the cause neither of justification nor of sanctification. Rather they are the fruits of God's favor toward us and the means by which we lay hold of the riches of God's mercy.[3]

There are encouraging signs that this lost dimension is being restored. Christian leaders from many denominations are reminding us that to be a *disciple* of Christ means to live under *discipline*. If we are to be saved from a weak, ineffectual Christianity, one of the means will be a restoration of disciplined living.

Some reply to any talk of discipline with the cry, "Legalism!" It is true that disciplines can become legalistic when they are enforced from the outside or when they are seen as a way to earn God's favor or to climb up some ladder to God. No spiritual discipline will establish our relationship to God. That has already been done by Christ through his incarnation, atonement, and resurrection—and by giving us the Holy Spirit. But disciplines freely chosen as a response to God result not in slavery, but in righteous liberty.

Some shrink away from self-discipline simply because it is hard, especially in our permissive culture. Discipline goes contrary to the spirit of our times and to the desires of the flesh which call for instant success, instant solutions, instant health, and instant spiritual maturity through one blazing experience. For that reason I'm convinced we need to recover what Richard Foster calls "the celebration of discipline."[4]

Spiritual disciplines, this Quaker writer points out, are not just for super Christians; they are for all of us.

> We must not be led to believe that the Disciplines are for spiritual giants and hence beyond our reach, or for contemplatives who devote all their time to prayer and meditation. Far from it. God intends the Disciplines of the spiritual life to be for ordinary human beings: people who have jobs, who care for children, who must wash dishes and mow lawns. In fact, the Disciplines are best exercised in the midst of our normal daily activities. If they are to have any transforming effect, the effect must be found in the ordinary junctures of human life: in our relationships with our husband or wife, our brothers and sisters, our friends and neighbors.[5]

Foster goes on to say that spiritual disciplines are not grim, teeth-clenching exercises, but adventures in joyful freedom.

> Neither should we think of the Spiritual Disciplines as some dull drudgery aimed at exterminating laughter from the face of the earth. Joy is the keynote of the Disciplines. The purpose of the Disciplines is liberation from the stifling slavery of self-interest and fear. When one's inner spirit is set free from all that holds it down, that can hardly be described as dull drudgery. Singing, dancing, even shouting characterize the Disciplines of the spiritual life.[6]

Henri Nouwen, writing in *Sojourners* magazine, stated:

> Precisely because our secular milieu offers us so few spiritual disciplines, we have to develop our own. We have, indeed, to fashion our own desert where we can withdraw every day, shake off our compulsions, and dwell in the gently healing presence of our Lord. Without such a desert we will lose our own soul while preaching the gospel to others. But with such a spiritual abode, we will become increasingly conformed to him in whose name we minister.
>
> The very first thing we need to do is set apart a time and a place to be with God and him alone. The concrete shape of the discipline of solitude will be different for each person.[7]

Spiritual discipline has not come easy for me. It has been a long, uphill struggle with many setbacks. There is a long way to go, but I rejoice with every gain I make. Each one makes the next step easier.

I have tried various forms of spiritual discipline, and one that has worked especially well for me is journal keeping. One proof of its significance is that I have kept at it for more than forty years.

I consider the time spent writing in my journal as sabbath time—a time of rest and solitude, a time to come apart to be with God and to reflect on the word, to search for the will, and to record the insights I receive. My journal has been the channel of many blessings.

I have many friends, too, who have found that the disciplin
journal writing seems right for our times and is suited to their pe
sonalities and needs.

In my teaching, I have seen that some people take to journal
keeping immediately. Others work into it gradually, and some never
find it very rewarding. Certainly those who enjoy expressing themselves in words will find it more natural.

Because of the benefits that can come from keeping a journal, I
invite you to try it.

Chapter 2

...periencing the Benefits of a Spiritual Journal

We have seen that the spiritual life is a process by which our entire lives are transformed more and more into the likeness of Christ. In the midst of this process is a paradox:

Our Christian walk is one of grace, yet certain disciplines are essential for our growth in grace. Paul realized that paradox when he wrote: "Continue to work out your salvation with fear and trembling, for it is God who works in you to will and to act according to his good purpose" (Phil. 2:12-13).

Keeping a spiritual journal is one of those practices whereby we may grow in grace. As I've reflected on my own use of a journal and talked with others about theirs, I've identified ten common benefits of journal keeping.

1. Growth in self-understanding
D. Martyn Lloyd-Jones has written:

> There is nothing which is quite so important as that we should without delay, and as quickly as possible, get to know ourselves. For the fact of the matter is that though we are all Christians together, we are all different, and the problems and the difficulties, the perplexities and the trials that we are likely to meet are in a large measure determined by the differences of temperament and of type.[1]

If we are to be useful to God and to other people, we need to know ourselves, our temperaments, our gifts, our strengths, and our weaknesses. This is no easy process. The apostle James wrote of the man "who looks at his face in a mirror and, after looking at himself, goes away and immediately forgets what he looks like" (James 1:23-24). Keeping a journal can be a way to avoid that kind of forgetfulness as we record the personal insights we have gained.

Writing in a journal can also help us be more honest with ourselves. One friend told me, "Writing in my journal helps me be truthful. If I write something false about my life, I can't get by with it. My rationalizing stands out when I see it in black and white."

Some Christian writers have minimized or even condemned the search for self-understanding. They see the self as the enemy of God. Although there can be a wrong kind of self-centeredness and self-absorption, I believe journal keeping can actually help free us from that by making us more aware of our own thinking and acting.

Elizabeth O'Connor responds forcefully to those who criticize self-exploration:

> When we discourage persons from being on an inward journey of self-discovery, we keep them from coming into possession of their own souls, keep them from finding the eternal city, keep them from being authentic persons who use their gifts and personality to mediate God's peace and God's love. He or she who tries to keep another from the pilgrim path of self-discovery is doing the devil's work.[2]

Keeping a spiritual journal can provide the time and the structure for exploring our lives—our thoughts, our feelings, our dreams, our relationships with others and with God, our gifts, our beliefs. It can increase our awareness of God's leading and action in our lives.

In *Spiritual Rx,* Frederic and Mary Ann Brussat explain how a journal can aid in self-understanding:

> Writing regularly in a journal encourages you to become a "watcher," to check up on your own behavior and to monitor your attitudes. All the spiritual traditions teach that it is difficult to change, to grow in wisdom, unless you first recognize who you are and how you habitually act.[3]

2. An aid to caring for your soul

Most of us believe in the value of a regular time of Bible reading, meditation, and prayer—or at least we have a nagging feeling that we *ought* to have such a time. We make good resolutions and succeed for a time, only to fall back into desultory habits. In our busy and fragmented lives, we need help to maintain these basic Christian disciplines. A journal can provide this help.

One of the biggest stumbling blocks to maintaining a regular devotional time is the difficulty of moving from an overstimulating environment into the calm stillness necessary for prayer and devotion. For me, writing is a focusing act, a great aid to concentration.

In *Freedom of Simplicity*, Richard Foster writes:

> A journal has the added merit of focusing and concentrating our thinking. Writing out our concerns helps to clarify things and keep us honest. Self-centered prayers become manifestly self-centered, even to us, when seen on paper. Insights that are hazy figures on the horizon sometimes become crystal clear when committed to a journal. Vacillating indecision can be turned into marching orders.[4]

In addition to focusing our attention, the act of writing can also generate ideas. One friend says, "I find writing in my journal fruitful. Something happens when I write. Fresh thoughts come to me that I would not otherwise have."

3. Guidance and decision making

As Christians, we want our lives to conform to God's will. We know that God wants the best for us. In some areas of our lives we have clear guidance from God's word, but in many specific areas of life, discerning God's will is more difficult. For example, we know God wants us to choose a life's work that honors him and serves others. But what we are specifically called to do is often not as clear. We need to do extensive exploring to uncover our "sealed orders."

I once heard someone say, "We find out what we think when we talk." I agree, but I find out even more about myself when I write.

Not only do I find out what I am thinking, but I often discover where God is directing me and what God has to say to me.

When we're faced with a decision, we can weigh the alternatives in our journal before making the decision. Then, because we have a record of the whole process, we can later recall why we decided as we did. This may help us find strength to carry out our resolve.

4. Making sense and order of life

Psychologist Victor Frankl, who survived the Nazi death camps, has declared that one of our great needs in life is to find meaning, to make sense and order of our lives. We need answers to the questions, "What's it all about?" "What am I doing here?" "What is my life for?"

Novelist R. V. Cassill writes:

> Writing is not merely a profession. It is a way of coming to terms with the world and with oneself. The whole spirit of writing is to overcome narrowness and fear by giving order, measure, and significance to the flux of experience constantly dinning into our lives. Out of that din comes fear of ignorance, fear of being alone, fear of dying without having defied the brutal indifference of the physical universe. Everyone who writes makes some attempt to face those fears by the very act of writing as best he can.[5]

I find that after a hectic day or a week loaded with events and people and problems, I gain a great sense of peace by sitting down with my journal in the presence of God and sorting out my life and regaining my perspective. It's like walking into a messy room—toys and clothes and books piled around—and slowly picking things up and putting them into their right places again. Then the room "feels good," and I can go on living there. In a similar way, my journal helps me sort out things in my life and restore some internal order.

Many people begin keeping journals because they feel this need to make sense of their lives. A college student writes: "I started my journal in my senior year in high school. At the time I was very frustrated at things going on around me, and I found that writing down my thoughts and feelings helped clarify them, and also released the tension inside me in a positive way."

5. Releasing emotions and gaining perspective

A variety of feelings surge within us: happiness, anger, depression, joy, jealousy, fear, thankfulness. Healthy-minded Christians must recognize these feelings and find ways to handle them. If we don't, these feelings will handle us, leading us to do things we don't want to do or preventing us from doing things we know we should do.

A journal can help us handle our emotions. First of all, we can diffuse emotions by expressing them in writing. Bottling up emotions, especially negative ones like anger or depression, only makes them worse. If we try to ignore them because we think "Christians shouldn't feel that way," we may be setting ourselves up for a major emotional crisis.

We need to find safe ways to express our negative emotions—ways that do not harm us or others. Instead of acting on impulse and lashing out at our children or our spouses or our co-workers, we can write out the anger in our journal. Perhaps you've had the experience of writing a letter to someone, soundly telling them off, and then destroying the letter before it was mailed. The journal permits this same kind of release. One journal keeper says, "I write down my fury whenever I can't talk with whoever is driving me wild."

W. R. Inge, then dean of St. Paul's Cathedral in London, expressed in his diary his feelings about another prominent Christian:

> Like other people who are in the public eye, I have enemies. There is G. K. Chesterton, who certainly hates me, and is reported to have said that one of his reasons for becoming a Papist was that he could not remain in the same Church as the Dean of St. Paul's. I retaliated in my diary by hoping that the public would soon get tired of the elephantine capers of an obese mountebank. These flowers of speech happily did not find their way into print.[6]

(Later Dean Inge changed his mind, and the words did get into print!)

After we have diffused a negative emotion like anger, we can go back and analyze, "Why did I react that way?" "Do I need to change in some way?" "Can I alter the situation so that a similar blowup doesn't happen again?"

In *Letters to Scattered Pilgrims*, Elizabeth O'Connor identifies one benefit of writing out our emotions in a journal:

> Those of us who keep journals will be in better control of our tongues when we have written out some of the hurts and offenses we have suffered and when we have given expression to feelings of mistrust or revenge toward persons who are close to us, or with whom we would like to feel close. If we use journals to explore the intensity of tender and hateful feelings, we will find ourselves becoming better communicators. Expressive and appropriate words will be available when the time comes. The clearer we are about our feelings and desires, the better able we are to communicate them to others in a way they are able to understand.[7]

If a journal helps reduce negative emotions, it can reinforce positive ones. As we write about our joys and our achievements and our pleasures, we strengthen and reinforce them. Later, as we reread what we wrote, we can relive that positive emotion. As you will see in chapter 11, expressing those emotions leads to greater physical and mental health and well-being.

6. Greater awareness of daily life

"The glory of God is a human being who is fully alive," wrote St. Iranaeus in the second century. We have all known times when we have been fully alive—alert, aware, fully conscious. In *A Touch of Wonder*, Arthur Gordon refers to such moments:

> How do we keep in the forefront of our minds the simple fact that we live in an indescribably wonderful world? It's not easy. Routine

dulls the eye and ear. Repetition and familiarity fog the capacity for astonishment. Even so, moments come to all of us when everything suddenly seems fresh and new and marvelous. This gift of awareness makes possible some of our happiest hours. We need to be receptive to it and grateful for it.[8]

I believe that journal writing can help nourish this "gift of awareness" and make us more receptive to it.

At one time in my life I was doing watercolor painting. On days when I was painting I *saw* more. I was more aware of colors and textures and shapes. A friend who writes fiction says that when she is in the process of writing she is much more alert to people. She observes how they walk and talk. She notes the shape of their noses and the way they gesture.

Anne Morrow Lindbergh prayed in her diary:

God, let me be conscious of it! Let me be conscious of what is happening while it is happening. Let me realize it and feel vividly. Let not the consciousness of the event, as happens so often, come to me tardily, so that I miss half the experience. Let me be conscious of it![9]

Journal writing is an antidote to "spiritual sleepwalking." It can aid us in that basic Christian discipline of wakefulness. I'm impressed with the number of times in the Gospels that Jesus says, "Wake up! Be alert! Watch!" Your journal can keep you more aware of what is going on inside you and around you. It will make you alert to the stirrings of the Holy Spirit within you. It will keep you alive and growing.

7. Self-expression and creativity

"In the beginning God created . . . ," and we who are made in God's image can also be creators. We create in many ways—through writing, composing, drawing, woodworking, sewing, cooking, management, and childrearing. "Nothing feeds the center like creative work," wrote Anne Morrow Lindbergh.

I once read the statement "Impression without expression leads to depression." The opposite of this is "Impression with expression leads to joy." Journal writing is one form of creativity, and it can be a relaxing, joyful experience. It provides a nonthreatening environment, free of criticism, in which to exercise creativity.

In her book *Write to Discover Yourself,* Ruth Vaughn says:

> Creative writing is valuable for its own sake. It will broaden, deepen, intensify your relationship with yourself. It can be your most vital, viable release, recording, refiner of life's experiences.
>
> Creative writing is valuable for its own sake. It will broaden, deepen, intensify your relationship with your God. It can be your most vital, viable, examining experience, exulting in worship and wonder.
>
> Creative writing is valuable for its own sake. It will broaden, deepen, intensify your relationship with others. It can be your most vital, viable way of saying: "I care about you!" "Let's heart-share!" "Learn from me." "I LOVE YOU!"[10]

As you write in your journal, you will develop greater ease and fluency in writing. This may one day lead you to try writing for publication in a magazine or a local newspaper or even to write a book. A journal is a great training ground for the writer, and the experiences and thoughts captured there can be the raw material for many articles or stories.

8. Clarifying what you believe

Through books and magazines, radio and TV, and personal contacts, we are exposed to a myriad of contradictory beliefs about life, about God, about the human condition, about right and wrong. Even within the Christian church we are confronted with competing theologies and spiritualities. New ideas and fresh perspectives can be good, but sometimes in confusion and bewilderment we cry out, "What can I believe? What do I believe?"

E. Stanley Jones underlines the importance of answering these questions when he says, "1 know that a faith which does not hold my intellect will soon not hold my heart." By keeping a journal, we can take time to think through and clarify our beliefs.

Elton Trueblood describes how this happens for him:

> The very act of writing can be remarkably creative. When I sit down with the paper in front of me, I know in general what I want to say, but I seldom know the details. As the ideas are expressed in written form, however, they begin to grow and to develop by their own inherent logic. Always I am a bit surprised by what has been written, for I have become in some sense an instrument.[11]

Clarifying our beliefs in a journal can also help us follow Peter's instruction: "Always be prepared to give an answer to everyone who asks you to give the reason for the hope that you have" (1 Pet. 3:15). As we bring our beliefs into focus, we will have greater courage and ability to share the hope we have in Christ.

9. Setting goals and managing your time

In the last few years I have discovered the joys of setting and reaching goals. This process has revolutionized my life and has brought me a new sense of self-fulfillment.

Paul wrote to the Romans: "Don't let the world around you squeeze you into its own mold, but let God remold your minds from within, so that you may prove in practice that the plan of God for you is good, meets all his demands and moves toward the goal of true maturity" (Rom. 12:2 PHILLIPS). One way to put this scripture passage into effect is to have clear goals before you. You can use your journal to keep your goals before you, to clarify them, and to move toward reaching them.

Closely connected with goal setting is the process of time management. You can also use your journal to evaluate your present use of time and to organize your time more efficiently in order to make steady progress toward your goals.

10. *Working through problems*
In the normal course of life we face a succession of problems—at work, at home, in our relationships, in church life. In a journal we can "talk out" a problem, gain perspective on it, and sooner or later find a God-pleasing solution.

A journal is not a substitute for people, but the journal can become a friend and confidant, especially when we have no person to talk with. It can also save us from making a nuisance of ourselves by dumping our problems too consistently on someone else. And even if we do not find the answer to our problem through journal writing, it can help us gain enough clarity so that if we do decide to talk with a friend or counselor, we will be better prepared to do so.

Other Uses of the Journal

These ten benefits of journal keeping have to do with one's personal life. Some people also make good use of a journal in connection with their work or professional life.

A teacher can jot down notes at the end of each day regarding certain students and their needs, identifying learning activities that succeeded and analyzing problem areas that need work. When I was teaching at a school for missionary children, I tried to record each day what I called the "golden moments"—when Michel got excited about a book, or when Pier did a particularly good job of writing, or when the advanced writing class was caught up in a stimulating discussion. Later I could look back on these recorded moments for stimulation and encouragement.

A counselor might want to keep a written record of conferences with each client, a summary of what each person said, and the counselor's reactions to the sessions. Between sessions, the counselor could jot down thoughts in preparation for the next conference.

Douglas J. Rumford, pastor of the Presbyterian Church of Old Greenwich, Connecticut, writes:

The journal is also a tool I've used in counseling. When people are unclear concerning God's will or caught in a particular problem, I often encourage them to prayerfully talk it over with the Lord in a journal. This proved so helpful to one woman that she frequently counsels her friends to do the same. One day this woman learned that her nephew was distraught over the death of a teenaged friend in a boating accident. As she consoled him, she suggested he talk it out with God on paper. He did, and it helped him immensely to recognize his grief and renew his faith in the Lord.[12]

Anyone involved in writing or speaking can make excellent use of a journal. Here is a place to record and work out ideas, to copy quotations, to record snatches of dialogue.

Because a pastor combines the roles of teacher, counselor, and speaker, he or she can use the journal in all of the above ways.

One pastor I know does his sermon preparation in his journal. On Monday morning he chooses the text for next Sunday's sermon. In a spirit of prayer, he meditates on the Scripture passage and records his thoughts and prayers. Then on Tuesday he reads what he has written and adds new thoughts. He repeats the process every day. By the end of the week, he usually has enough material for two or three sermons. "It's a way of holding the word of God for an extended period of time," he says. "It helps me sustain myself in the word and the word in me."

Preserving a Journal

For me, a journal has value as *process* as well as *product*. There are beliefs that come from the process of writing—the aid to concentration, the focusing of the mind, the generating of ideas—even if one were to throw the writing away immediately.

But there are added benefits if our writing is preserved for later rereading and further reflection. The journal is valuable as a product. It gives us a permanent record of our thoughts and our lives.

Douglas Rumford writes:

As we reflect on our spiritual pilgrimage, we gain understanding of the dynamics of spiritual life: the obstacles, the predictable crises, the doubts, and the means of grace to overcome these. The preservation of these insights and the memory of God's faithfulness promotes an attitude of praise and thanksgiving. . . .

A favorite motto of my ministry is "Write it down." When someone tells me of answered prayer, an exciting evangelistic encounter, or an insight into Scripture, I urge them to write it down. As a result, many in our congregation, especially among the leaders, have begun keeping journals. A new appreciation has grown for the fact of God's activity in the details of our lives.[13]

Kathryn Koob, an American held hostage in Iran for more than a year, kept a journal there. Writing on the back of envelopes, she jotted down a record of her days in captivity. "My journal helped me remember my reactions and some things I had read," she said. "It also reminded me of things I wanted to think about more deeply and helped crystallize my thinking."

If we choose to do so, we can preserve our journals even beyond our lifetime. They may then provide inspiration and enjoyment for generations to come.

The Christian church has been enriched by spiritual leaders who have left in their journals a record of their lives with God, their spiritual insights, and their reflections on the Scriptures. We have the journals of John Wesley, George Whitefield, John Woolman, David Brainerd, Blaise Pascal, David Livingstone, Thomas Merton, Francis Asbury, and many others. We can say about each of them, "By faith he still speaks, even though he is dead" (Heb. 11:4).

No Age Barrier

One of the great things about journal keeping is that it can be done at any age.

Children can start as soon as they can write, or even earlier if a parent writes their words for them. Some schools encourage children to keep a journal as a way of teaching self-expression.

When my daughter, Rebecca, was eight years old, I bought her a journal. I explained to her why I keep one, and told her about the kinds of material she could put into it. To help her establish the habit of journaling, I offered to pay her a nickel for each page she wrote. (If she wrote every day, it would cost me about eighteen dollars a year, a price I was more than willing to pay!)

I've taught journal writing to teenagers, many of whom took to it immediately. It came at a time in their lives when they were beginning to think for themselves and develop their own philosophies of life. The journal became a confidant, a safe place to work out ideas and to express the tumultuous feelings of early adolescence. Some of these students are now in college and continue to maintain their journals.

People also go on writing journals in their seventies and eighties and beyond. Life gives them more time for reflection, and they may especially enjoy savoring the past, perhaps leaving a record of their life's journey for their children and grandchildren.

By now you might be convinced there are indeed many benefits to be gained by journal writing. But how do you get started?

Chapter 3

Getting Started

Although journal writing would have value as a process even if you were to throw away what you wrote, it has even greater value if you preserve your writing. For this reason it is better to use a journal that is bound in some way, rather than writing on loose scraps of paper. Beyond that, the form of the journal is a matter of personal preference.

My friend Allan uses a small looseleaf notebook. "I chose this form to allow me to 'edit' (that means 'destroy') pages if I want. Thus far I have thrown nothing away."

Greg, a college student interested in creative writing, says, "I keep my journal in a dog-eared red folder along with poems and stories I'm writing, which also act as records of my life."

Another friend says, "I write in lovely hardbound books with quality paper and attractive covers. They're called 'Empty Books.'"

Be sure you use a journal that is large enough. The typical schoolgirl diary with a tiny lock provides only a few inches for each entry. And most dated diaries, even the largest, do not provide adequate space for a thorough journal.

So that leads us to some form of blank book. One problem with expensive bound books, besides cost, is that they may be so elegant that they inhibit your writing. You may be afraid to "mess them up," or you may be too concerned with conserving space to write freely.

Some people prefer a looseleaf notebook, and it does have some advantages. You can rearrange material if you want some order other than chronological. You can write on a loose page and insert it in the notebook later. You can use dividers and create a journal with several sections to keep similar entries together. For example, you could have a separate section for work or for notes on your reading or for a nature journal. The main disadvantage is a practical one: It's hard to keep the pages in the notebook. Also, you may be tempted to destroy pages, but later wish you had kept them.

A narrow-lined 8½ x 11-inch spiralbound notebook works best for me. I feel comfortable writing in one, and each notebook gives me enough space for about three months of writing. When I finish each volume, I place it with others in a ring binder. A row of these bound volumes now stands on the bookshelves in my study, holding forty years of my journals in sequence.

Some people like a smaller notebook, one that fits more easily into purse or pocket so they can jot down thoughts at odd moments. However, I still prefer the larger size, as I don't generally carry my journal around unless I'm on a vacation or a trip. If I have some idea or quotation I want to capture while I'm away from home, I jot it on some scrap of paper and later transfer it into my journal.

Some people dress up a plain notebook with a colored picture from a calendar or magazine, individualizing the journal and setting a peaceful mood for reflection and writing.

An unlined notebook seems to give some people greater freedom. These people may include drawings or doodles, and they sometimes write in corners or in little groupings across the page. I feel more comfortable with the structure of lines, but I plan to try an unlined book sometime to see if it makes any difference in the way I write.

Obviously, you will want to experiment to find out which notebook feels right for you, until you settle on one in which you write comfortably and regularly.

Two alternatives to handwriting a journal are typing it and tape-recording it.

I still prefer writing in my journal the old-fashioned way—by hand, but other people prefer writing their journal on their computer. Today's laptops are convenient and portable. A word-processed entry can be copied and e-mailed to a friend or family member. It is also easy to keep various kinds of entries in different files for easy access.

If you write your journal on a computer, please remember to back up your files to disk or print out a hard copy.

One friend, when he's especially busy, finds he can record his thoughts on tape more quickly and easily than he can write. He also tapes while he's driving, thus making good use of that time. The problem with tapes is that it is harder to locate specific items when you want them. My friend later transcribes his tapes, but admits he often falls behind

All these variations are worth exploring, depending on your temperament and the conditions under which you are most likely to do your journaling. As you work with your journal, you'll find a way that's best for you.

One or More Journals?

Many people record everything in one journal—daily thoughts, observations, quotations, clippings, and so on. The journal, then, is a unifying force in their lives; everything comes together in one place.

Others find it helpful to have several journals. Here are some examples.

1. Notes on books

If you do a significant amount of reading and want to take notes, you may find it handy to keep the notes for a particular book in one place, rather than scattered through many days' recordings in your journal.

Occasional quotes from magazines or sermons go into my regular journal, but I keep a special journal for book notes. I number the pages in the notebook and reserve the first page as a table of contents. So, for example, I might have on the contents page: "pp. 1-16, Henri Nouwen, *Reaching Out.*"

2. Family journal

One woman I know keeps a family journal in addition to her personal journal. In it she keeps a record of the children's development and some of their sayings and observations, preserving family memories.

I recently heard of a mother who keeps a journal on her learning-disabled child. She records the activities used to help him and details his progress.

One family keeps an open family journal in which any member, adult or child, may write.

3. Dream journal

Some people who are convinced their dreams are a significant source of personal insight keep a dream log at their bedside. When they awaken, they immediately jot down their dream and any thoughts they have as to its meaning. Later, as they reflect on the dream, they write what they think they can learn from it. I try to at least record what I remember of dreams that are especially striking. If you want to know more about dreams and a dream journal, read *The Inward Adventure* by Morton Kelsey (Augsburg, 1980).

4. Work journal

You might find it desirable to keep your work records separate from your personal journal. Because my work of writing is so closely related to the rest of my life, I prefer keeping both together. Upon reviewing a journal volume, I index the items pertaining to my work and transfer them to other notebooks kept specifically for my writing.

5. Nature journal

I have a separate notebook—with a green cover, of course—in which to keep a record of my observation of birds and animals and notes on my gardening. More on this in chapter 4.

6. Project journal

When I'm working on a long-term project, like writing a book, I keep a special daily record, listing what I did each day and jotting ideas for next steps. This allows me to monitor my progress and keeps me moving forward. A similar method could work for any sort of ongoing task in which you need to chart your way.

Finding Time to Write

"I'd like to keep a journal, but I just never find time for it." That's probably the most commonly heard problem about journaling. The only reply to that excuse is that we always have enough time for what we think is really important. If you become convinced of the value of journal keeping, you will organize your priorities to make room for it. Even the busiest of us can find fifteen minutes or half an hour to set aside for journal writing.

I believe in the "wedge principle" of time management. When splitting a log, one first drives a wedge in a short distance. Then the wedge can be driven in farther. If you establish the habit of writing for fifteen minutes a day, you can go on to half an hour or longer if you feel the need or desire.

I believe people will benefit most when they write in a journal daily. A certain rhythm of reflection and writing is established. Even the words *journal* or *diary* mean a "daybook," carrying the thought of daily writing.

It is not necessary to write daily, however. Some people find it more natural to write weekly or just occasionally. Many of my friends find their journal valuable even though they only write sporadically. Allan says, "I'm terribly undisciplined about writing in my journal. I usually wait until some major event occurs that I want to remember. Or I work through some problem and the insight is worth remembering. This happens every week or two."

"I wish I could say I write every day," Pat said, "but for some reason I forget, especially if my schedule changes. In past years, I sometimes avoided writing in it because things were either too painful or very wonderful. I now regret that it didn't seem necessary to record those times. These past years I try to write whenever I remember, no matter how I feel, and it's much more helpful."

For years I kept a journal irregularly. I would write every day for months, then skip days, weeks, or even months. I began daily writing in earnest when we moved to Madagascar, and I felt it important to capture the details of this unique experience of living in the Third World. Now the habit is so firmly set that my day seems off balance or incomplete unless I write in my journal.

If you are convinced you cannot write in a journal every day, I still recommend that you keep one. Write in it when you can. A general rule might be to *write frequently enough so that nothing significant is lost.*

When to Write

Journal keeping is a highly individual matter. There is no "right" way to do it. You will have to examine your own schedule and do the writing when you can fit it in.

When you are beginning to keep a journal, it is helpful to write at the same time every day. That way a habit is established, and you'll find it easier to do. The "creative juices" will begin to flow at a certain time each day. However, if it is not possible for you to write at the same time each day, then write whenever you can.

Morning and evening seem to lend themselves naturally to journal writing. If you write in the morning, you can reflect on the events of the previous day and then use the journal to plan and prepare for the day ahead. Morning is a particularly good time for working on goal setting (see chapter 6).

The end of the day is a natural time for looking back on the events of the day and sorting out what is significant. Evening is also a traditional time for the "examination of conscience," for taking an honest look at where we have fallen short of God's will, and asking for forgiveness and transformation. Some people like to use the evening to plan the next day's work. When I do that, I tend to stay awake thinking about it, so I reserve my planning for the morning.

If neither of these times works for you, perhaps because of family or work responsibilities, look for other time slots. A mother might write when her baby takes a nap. An office worker might write during the lunch hour. A teacher might find time to write after school, when the classroom is finally empty. A college student could use the break between classes.

On some days I write in my journal three or four times, whenever things come up that I want to record. Other times I write only once, usually first thing in the morning. My friend Dorothée says, "I usually write in my journal at night before I go to bed, but there have been times when I carried my journal with me and wrote off and on during the day. Sometimes I'll write as many as five times a day—and sometimes I won't write for months. It depends on my mood, and if I can express myself in other ways."

In summary, find *some* time that works for you. Experiment with writing at various times of the day. Write every day if you can, but don't force yourself. It is better to write occasionally than not at all.

Conditions for Writing

The ideal situation is to have some quiet spot where you can write regularly. When your mind realizes that you are in your writing place, it is more likely to move into writing gear and start producing. I have a favorite chair by a window that allows me to look out at my gardens between paragraphs. Some people like to write in bed, others at a table or desk. One woman found that the best place for her to write was on the basement steps, with the doors closed at both ends.

Perhaps a record or tape in the background may help set a mood for reflection. For many people, instrumental music is better than songs with words.

Once you've established the habit of journal writing, you will probably be able to do it anywhere. I've written in bus depots, on airplanes, on trains, outdoors, and in various locations in the house.

Experiment. Try out various places until you find one that is comfortable for you.

How Much to Write

Abraham Lincoln was once asked how long a man's legs should be. He answered, "Long enough to reach the ground." One could give a similar answer to the question, "How much should I write every day?" Write as much as you need or want to.

Some days I write only four or five lines. Other days I write that many pages. Much depends on my schedule and on how much is going on in my life—outwardly or inwardly.

At first you might set yourself a time limit: "I will write for at least fifteen minutes." Or you could try setting a certain goal—say half a page or a page a day.

Some people have too much to write. They feel it would take them two or three hours a day, so they don't even start. If this is your problem, you might want to set a maximum time: "For the next half hour I'll try to catch as much of this as I can." Then jot down the highlights and main ideas. Don't worry about details; capture as much as you can now. You can always add details later.

Getting Started

If you're just beginning a journal, you may feel awkward as you face that blank page. You may feel self-conscious, wondering, "Who am I to be keeping a journal?" These are natural feelings.

The best way to get over them is just to start writing. Don't worry about your spelling or grammar. Don't try to evaluate your writing style. Don't worry about the profundity of your thoughts. Stop comparing yourself to C. S. Lewis—or worse yet, to St. Paul! Turn off the critical voices within you and just write. The thoughts may not be very profound, but they are *your* thoughts. The words may not be very eloquent, but they are *your* words.

A student once asked a college professor, "How can I get started studying when I don't feel like it?" The professor answered, "Go through the *motions,* and you'll get the *emotions.*" I find the same is true for writing. Take up your pen and start writing, whether you feel like it or not, and the words will come.

The problem for most of us is that our education developed the *critical* part of our minds at the expense of our *creative* faculties. So when we sit down to write, we are stifled by thoughts like "This isn't very good," or "I wonder if this is the right way to do this," or "What would Mrs. Jones think of this?"

But you cannot create and criticize at the same time. When you're creating, you must by an act of the will turn off the critic. And a journal provides an ideal place for doing that.

One way to turn off the critic is by practicing what is called *flow*-writing or *free*-writing.

Exercise in Flow-Writing

Some people find that the practice of flow-writing helps loosen them up. In flow-writing, you stop judging what you write and just let the words flow. The only rule is that you must write steadily, nonstop, for ten minutes. If you get temporarily stuck, describe the room you're in, repeat a word or a sentence, or write "I can't think of anything to say" or "This is a stupid exercise!" Anything. Just keep writing and don't look back or change what you've written. Just keep the writing flowing.

At the end of ten minutes, you will have a very tired hand, but you will also have filled several pages with words. To be sure, much of it will not be worth saving. The point is that you have written that much, and you have loosened up, like an athlete loosening up before a game.

This is a good exercise if you are a particularly perfectionistic person or if you are uptight about writing. It is also good when you want to write, but your mind is cluttered. Ten minutes of flow-writing can free you up and settle you down so you can write more clearly in your journal.

You can do the flow-writing in your journal, but you might not want to waste the pages on that low level of writing. When I feel the need to do flow-writing, I write on scrap paper. Before I throw the scraps away, I read through them and salvage any sentences or ideas that I want to retain in my journal.

If you have a hard time getting started at writing, try flow-writing for ten minutes a day for a few weeks to see if it loosens you up. One prominent teacher of writing, Peter Elbow, recommends flow-writing as a major method for developing greater writing freedom and power.

You might want to consult his books, *Writing without Teachers* (Oxford University Press, 1998) and *Writing with Power* (Oxford University Press, 1998).[1]

Your Personal Contract

To begin your journal, you may want to write a statement of why you want to experiment with journaling. For example:

I'm starting this journal because I want to grow spiritually. My goal is to understand myself better and to clarify what I believe. I think a journal will help by providing a framework for reflection and a place to record my thoughts and experiences.

Then, underneath the statement you might want to write a contract with yourself: *"Therefore, I contract with myself, and before God, to spend at least fifteen minutes a day writing in my journal,"* or *". . . to write at least a few lines in my journal every day,"* or *". . . to write at least one hour a week."*

After recording your reasons for journal keeping, you will probably want to begin with what I consider the heart of the journal—the Daily Record.

Chapter 4

The Daily Record

One of my favorite early television programs was the historical documentary *You Are There.* I still remember the announcer at the end of the program intoning, "What kind of a day was it? A day like all days—filled with those events that alter and illuminate our time—and *you were there!*"

Our lives are spelled out in days, and in our journals we can ask the question, "What were the events that altered and illuminated *my* time?"

To answer that question we might choose to record a variety of things. The following list suggests the range of material that might go into a journal. Don't let the list overwhelm you. You certainly will not write about every one of these topics every day.

1. Personal events

The most basic level of the journal is "What did I do today?" or "What happened to me today?" I always include that in my journal— even the everyday details of going to the store, or taking a hike, or working in the garden.

On a particularly hectic day that seems to have been a whirlwind, I find it helps to sort out and list just what took place. Even as simple a thing as making a list is a first step in making sense and order out of the day.

Then I try to write freely about it, without worrying about getting it all right. This spontaneous, uncalculated writing is what gives a diary unique freshness.

In a diary you catch the excitement of each event because the emotion is fresh. The diary is spontaneous, uncalculated, and persuasive because the event has just occurred. The sense of immediacy is the value of a diary and gives the feeling of newly discovered truth.[1]

You can catch the feeling of immediacy in this account from John Wesley's journal.

Sunday, July 1, 1745
I preached, at five, to a quiet congregation, and about eight, at Stithians. Between six and seven in the evening we came to Tolcarn. Hearing the mob was rising again, I began preaching immediately. I had not spoken a quarter of an hour before they came in view. One Mr. Trounce rode up first and began speaking to me, wherein he was roughly interrupted by his companions. Yet, as I stood on a high wall and kept my eyes upon them, many were softened and grew calmer and calmer; which some of their companions observing, went round and suddenly pushed me down. I lit on my feet without any hurt; finding myself close to the warmest of the horsemen, I took hold of his hand and held it fast while I expostulated the case. As for being convinced, he was quite above it; however, both he and his fellows grew much milder, and we parted very civilly.[2]

One way to capture the immediacy of an event is to record the sensory details: What did you *see?* What did you *hear?* What did you *feel?* What did you *smell?* What did you *taste?* Reading details like these will help to recreate the experiences for you many years later.

2. Reactions to events
Your journal will be of more value to you if you move beyond the level of *what* happened to record your *reactions* to what happened. What did you think about the event? How did you feel about it?

Compare the following journal entries—two views of the same event:

Went to the store after supper and bought groceries. Came home and put them away.

*   *   *   *   *

Lyn volunteered to put the kids to bed if I would go grocery shopping. So I drove to the supermarket with her list. Although many people are constantly complaining about prices, my honest reaction is just plain gratitude. I still haven't gotten to the point where I take things for granted. I'm just happy we can buy fresh milk for the children and cheese for us. Maybe that's one of the best results for us of our years in Madagascar. We don't take as much for granted and feel more gratitude.

At the store I noticed an old couple shopping together. They were fussing and fretting at one another the whole time, like two children. Then I noticed a young couple, maybe newlyweds, doing some of their first shopping together and obviously treasuring every minute of it.

The first entry is a dry recital of facts. The second, although not great literature, gives more of a feeling of life because it includes some thoughts and observations. It finds some *meaning* in even a simple event.

3. Conversations

Some of the significant times in our lives happen in conversations, especially those that get beyond surface chatter. When people reveal something significant about themselves, or when we succeed in sharing some of our deeper feelings, these moments are worth recording. And this practice can make us better listeners.

We can do this in one of two ways. We can simply summarize, like this:

> While walking along the beach with Guy for two hours, Guy told me about his childhood in France, and then being evacuated to North Africa during World War II. He learned to speak English in order to beg from American soldiers. In some ways our backgrounds are similar—urban blue-collar backgrounds.

A second way would be to try to reproduce exactly what was said, as a novelist or playwright does. This is excellent practice for anyone interested in writing short stories or plays.

After a long, interesting discussion, I enjoy the sifting-out process: What did we talk about? What points were made? How did the conversation feel? Sometimes I look back on a long conversation and realize that little or nothing of any significance was said. That tells me something, too!

In addition to conversations that include me, I sometimes record snatches of conversation I overhear, such as that between two people on a bus, or between one of my children and a playmate.

Mary Schramm recorded this conversation, which took place after she and her husband posted a NO HUNTING sign on their farm.

Today a truck drove up in the rain and the driver demanded of Mark that his parents come out and talk with him. Because John was gone, I went out to greet our visitor. He refused my invitation to come into the house, so the conversation proceeded with me standing in the rain, peering through a half-open truck window.

"I just want you to know," the heavily bearded man began, "that I have hunted on this property all my life, and I intend to keep doing so!"

I introduced myself and asked his name. "I don't have a name. They just call me number three," he mumbled.

"Oh, come," I smiled, "everyone has a name. You're certainly important enough to be called something other than number three."

Then I realized this must be the man neighbors had warned us about. I kept wishing John were around and felt foolish that my heart was beating so quickly.

He continued to reinforce his message. "I intend to come up here with my gun and dogs, and there ain't nothing you can do to stop me!"

"You're right," I said. "There is nothing I can do, but I would hope you would respect our wishes."

He didn't seem to hear and was shouting now. "You can shoot me or call the sheriff if you want, but I'm still going to hunt on this property!"

"No, we would never do that. We don't even own a gun. We only ask that you respect our NO HUNTING signs." I was very wet and shivering, but he seemed to be running out of steam. He began stretching and yawning, never looking me in the eye.

"Well, I can send my dogs across your land to drive the deer off and then shoot them on the other side of the line fence," he said.

"Yes, you could, but I don't think you will," I responded.

The man stared ahead for a few minutes, started his truck and mumbled as he rolled up his window. "Well, I certainly hope you'll be happy here. It's a good farm."

He drove off down the lane. We have seen him several times since. He comes to the farm occasionally to "look things over," but he never has his gun.[3]

4. Prayers

When writing about things of deep concern, it is natural for the Christian to turn words into prayer. If we're writing about happy events, we may be led to write brief words of praise and thanksgiving. Or we can write a longer prayer about the situation.

We don't have to attempt any kind of model prayers or literary masterpieces. We only need to write words from our own hearts. If we are writing about a problem or a friend or family member in pain, we may write a prayer of intercession, asking for God's help and committing the person to his care.

You will find more ideas about using a journal for prayer in chapter 7.

5. Questions

You can learn much about yourself by becoming more aware of the questions you are asking. Sometimes these questions are elusive, like butterflies. We have to catch them before they flit away. This is where a journal is useful.

What *are* the questions you are living day by day? They may be practical questions: "What am I going to do about the car?" "How can we make it financially?" They may be about relationships: "How can I get along better with Susan?" They may concern the direction of our lives: "Should I go back to school?" "Why do I feel depressed so much of the time?" "What does God want me to do with my life?" They may be theological questions: "How can I know what is true?" "Can I believe the miracle stories in the Bible?" "Does God really answer prayer?"

Our questions reveal where we are in our life's journey. By recognizing our questions and recording them, we have taken the first step toward answering them.

What questions occupy your mind? Are you aware of them? If you could ask God any ten questions and be guaranteed a clear answer, what would you ask? As you catch sight of your questions, jot them down—perhaps on a piece of scratch paper—and record them later in your journal. Then, in study and conversation, you can explore the answers.

6. Memories

The human mind is capable of maintaining a treasure store of rich memories. Some experts on the brain claim that everything we have ever done or heard or read is stored there, although we cannot always retrieve the information. Sometimes an event of the day triggers a memory of something we had not thought about for years or even decades. This memory then becomes a vivid event in the present.

A friend wrote this in her journal:

> At Good Friday services I experienced what I have heard people talk about before—how listening to talk about death and dying can be almost unbearably painful. Pastor Greg was talking about dying, and the last days I was with Mother before she died came flooding back to me so vividly that my jaws and teeth began to ache!

I wrote this memory in my journal:

> A bright cold frosty morning today. As I walked downtown I remembered my first day in Minneapolis twelve years ago. I had flown up from St. Louis the day before, leaving shirt-sleeve weather there. When Roland picked me up at the airport and took me to the Francis Drake Hotel, I stepped out into minus twenty-eight-degree cold and heaps of snow. The next morning I walked from the hotel to the Nicollet Mall on this kind of brilliant crisp morning, feeling at home, as if this were the right place for me (even though I had said I would never move north again!).

Much is being written today about roots and their importance, especially when so many people move frequently and are cut off from family and friends. A healthy sense of rootedness may be an important ingredient of mental and spiritual health. We can nourish our own sense of roots by writing about our memories, reclaiming those parts of our lives.

For more detailed and systematic approaches, you can do this "remembering" in a more deliberate way. You will find some ways to do this in chapter 8. Perhaps you will choose to write an autobiography for your own sake or for your family, or even for publication.

7. Insights

Psychologists refer to an insight as the "Aha!" experience, as when a light bulb appears above a character in a comic strip.

An insight may be a new understanding of yourself and why you act as you do. It may be an insight into another person or into your spiritual life. Perhaps it is a new solution to a problem at work or in the family. It may be a new appreciation of something you have been taking for granted.

By recording these insights, you not only preserve them but also, by making yourself more aware of your thoughts, enable valuable insights to come more often.

Elton Trueblood wrote of a visit he had with W. P. Faunce, president of Brown University:

> While we were talking on the subject, which was highly important for my career, I was shocked to see the great man suddenly stop speaking, take out a notebook, and write in it for three or four minutes, while I sat in silence. When he had finished writing, President Faunce again spoke to me, asking my pardon for this seeming discourtesy. Then he explained that ideas were his capital and that he had suddenly had an idea not connected with our immediate conversation. He went on to say that he had learned to put down ideas when they came because otherwise they might be lost forever. Far from being hurt, as he feared I might be, I was immensely grateful. With rare exceptions I have carried a notebook ever since and have learned that my ideas are not retained unless they are recorded.[4]

8. Joys

"To miss the joy is to miss all," wrote Robert Louis Stevenson.

Your joys are great gifts from God. These moments deserve to be treasured, pondered, relived, and cherished.

Remembering your joys helps you focus on the good life and helps keep you in a positive attitude. It's a good antidote to self-pity and depression.

Try this experiment for a few days. At the end of each day, ask yourself: "What were the most joyful moments of this day?" Then record them briefly. You will probably find that even the grimmest day has at least a few sparks of joy!

Over the past weeks I've found myself listing joys like these:
- Planting some native perennial sunflowers and liatris in the yard
- Sitting by a campfire along the Brule River with Lyn and Hans, reading aloud from the poems of Wendell Berry
- Harvesting tomatoes and chard and collard from the vegetable garden
- Singing old-time gospel music with Lee and Willie and Louise at the Barron County Fair

9. Gratitude journal

Closely related to the joys list is a gratitude list, a simple naming of the special blessings of the day. You might begin with the heading: "Five Things for Which I Am Especially Grateful Today," and then let your mind drift back over the day, the people, the activities, the gifts. Of course, you don't have to limit yourself to five, but setting a number creates a kind of game and promotes a playful attitude.

My gratitude list made me more aware of blessings like these:

- Meeting Rachel, who shares my birthday, at the Gasthaus Bavarian Hunter for German food and good conversation
- After three weeks of drought, an inch of rain
- The books I was able to find in used bookstores in Iowa City
- For the electrician who came and restored the power to our house
- For first copies of my new book *When Your Parent Dies* and for the friends who helped me write it

There's an old prayer that goes something like this: "O God, you have given me so much. I ask for one more thing: a grateful heart." Reviewing your gratitude lists at the end of a week or month is almost sure to raise your spirits and brighten your mood.

10. Achievements and failures

What do you think you have accomplished so far in life? If you were to die today, what would you feel good about having done? I think it is good for us to recognize what the Lord has enabled us to achieve in life. God did not intend for us to be miserable failures, and we are being falsely humble when we can't recognize what God is doing in the world through us.

By recognizing your achievements, you can celebrate them, thank God for them, heighten your confidence, and build on your successes.

Because my profession is writing, I note when I complete a writing project or when I receive an acceptance letter or an encouraging phone call from an editor. When I hear of someone being helped by something I've written, I record that, too. This is not to build my ego, but to give me the sense of worthwhileness about what I'm doing that will get me over the rough spots.

After a visit to a college campus I wrote this:

> A professor took me aside in the hall and said, "1 want to express our appreciation for your book, *Lord, I've Been Thinking.* Our son had been going through a tough time, and he said those prayers really helped him, and he said to me, "Dad, if you ever meet the author of that book again, tell him thanks from me." One story like this makes writing seem worthwhile.

Writing is lonely work and can often be discouraging. These kinds of memories remind me that writing is to serve others. Recording "achievements" like this helps give me the motivation to go on.

We can also record our failures—in work, in personal relationships, or in living up to our own commitments. We do this not with the thought of dwelling upon them and wallowing in misery, but to recognize them, confess them to God, and ask for forgiveness and the power to overcome them.

Someone has said that those who do not learn from history are bound to repeat it. This applies to our personal lives, too. The journal is a good place to ask, "What can I learn from this failure?" "How can I do things differently?" In this way we do not simply repeat mistakes, but find creative new ways to work out these problems.

11. World events

While our journals will probably focus on our personal lives, we live against the background of world history. The Bible presents God as actively involved not only in our private lives, but also in the affairs of nations. So when we study the historical events of the past or our own times, we are in some sense tracing the hand of God.

The extent to which you choose to write about public events will probably depend on your own interest in politics and current events, but you might want to at least record the events as they impinge on your life. For example, I made this entry in my journal:

November 22, 1963. I was showing a movie to my class when Lyn motioned for me to come out into the hall. I closed the door behind me. She looked really shaken and said, "One of the mothers just called to say the President has been shot in Dallas." I went back into the room, feeling dazed. As soon as the film was over, I led the kids back into the regular classroom and put the radio on my desk. They all sat perfectly still, with none of the usual fooling around. They must have been able to tell from my face that something was wrong. I tried to keep my voice steady and said, "We've just heard that President Kennedy has been shot, and we want to find out how he is." They sat in perfect silence as we heard the news unravel and finally learned that the president was dead. We listened until almost 3:30. Then we sang:

God bless our native land;
Firm may she ever stand
Through storm and night.
When the wild tempests rave,
Ruler of the wind and wave,
Do thou our country save
By thy great might.

Some years later I wrote this entry:

Paul and I went to the downtown library. As we walked into the lobby a crowd of people were standing, watching the TV. My first thought was, "Somebody must have been shot." We soon learned it was President Reagan. I felt nothing, nothing, except, "Well, it's happened again. What else is new?" Maybe that's the real tragedy: that we can hear that kind of news and feel nothing.

More recently, I wrote:

September 11, 2001. In the morning I was still sitting with my journal when Rebecca called from Iowa City to ask: "Are you listening to the news? Someone hijacked commercial airliners and crashed them into the World Trade Center and the Pentagon!"

I was dumbfounded. It seemed so unreal, like a B-grade Hollywood disaster movie. I hung up and turned on National Public Radio. Lyn and I listened in silence, trying to comprehend what had happened, then drove to town to watch television with David, who greeted us with the words "Stand steady in the Light."

We watched the TV news—the same images over and over of a plane smashing through a skyscraper in a ball of fire, two huge skyscrapers collapsing in clouds of dust and debris, the Pentagon on fire, crowds of panicked people running through the streets of Manhattan. When we couldn't stand it any longer, we drove home. Needing to do something sane, I picked vegetables in the garden, and we cooked two big batches of soup to put in the freezer to warm us in the long cold winter ahead.

Recording events like this, and our reactions to them, not only helps us to be more sensitive to what is going on in the world, but it can provide a valuable record for those who follow us. I sometimes fantasize about my great-great-grandchildren reading my journal to find out, "What did great-great-Grandpa feel about the Kennedy assassination?" Or "What was it like for them to live in Madagascar in the 1970s?"

For my part, I wish I could read the story of my ancestors' migration from Europe to the United States. But unfortunately, they left no records. Recently, my wife's aunt sent us a copy of a journal kept by a relative who fought in the Civil War. This made fascinating reading for us and forged a link with history for our children.

Here is an excerpt from the Civil War diary, written by a seventeen-year-old farmboy who responded to Lincoln's call for volunteers:

October 17, 1862. Today found us in Harrisburg where we donned the blue. After that we went to Stoneman's Switch, near Fredericksburg, where we joined our Regiment commanded by Col. S. Bowman of Berwick. We was there but a short time until our Captain Fribley came to us and, after calling us into line, said,

"Boys, tomorrow we expect to engage in a bloody conflict, right across the river from where we are now, so if you have any letters to write or prayers to say, do them now, for God alone knows where we may be tomorrow."

Augustine Birrell wrote of Wesley's *Journal:* "We can learn better from Wesley's *Journal* than from anywhere else what manner of man Wesley was, and the character of the times during which he lived and moved and had his being."[5] Similarly, historians have always used journals as valuable primary sources in studying the history of a period—and not only the journals of famous generals or kings or politicians, but those of the "little people" who experienced life on the daily level at that time and place in history. The bibliography at the end of this book suggests some fascinating examples of historical journals.

12. Your reading

It is also valuable and worthwhile to keep a record of your reading as signposts of your spiritual/intellectual journey. My Daily Record usually indicates what I read and at least some brief comments.

Finished rereading Merton's *Sign of Jonas,* the journal of his years at Gethsemani Abbey. Besides the insights into prayer and life with God, there are comments on writing that I understand better now.

The first page of my personal journal is left blank as a place to list the title and authors of books I read. This gives me a quick check on how much and what kind of reading I'm doing.

When I reread my journal, I find it interesting to see what I was reading at a certain period in my life—and what my impressions of these books were and how they influenced me.

Ernest Dimnet, in *The Art of Thinking,* writes:

The moment we realize that any thought, ours or borrowed, is pregnant enough not to be wasted, or original enough not to be likely to come back again, we must fix it on paper. Our manuscript should mirror our reading, our meditations, our ideals, and our approach to it in our lives. Anybody who has early taken the habit to record himself in that way knows that the loss of his papers would also mean a loss of his thinking possibilities.[6]

13. Quotations

Often a significant truth about life is wrapped up in some few, well-chosen words. Haven't you had the experience of reading something especially well said in a magazine or book, and then later wishing you had written those words down? You can capture an idea and store it for further thought by copying it into your journal.

When I run across a good quote in my reading, or in a sermon or on radio or TV. I usually jot it down immediately. If my journal is not handy, I scribble on any available scrap of paper and then transfer it later. (As I mentioned earlier, I keep more substantive book notes in a separate notebook.)

It's good to establish the habit of writing down the source as well as the quote. This is especially true if you plan to use the quotation in some form of published writing.

14. Letters

Because letters often record the events of our lives, our personal vision, and our thoughts and ideas, some people incorporate them into their journals. This can be done in several ways. If you regularly type your letters, you can make a photocopy or another printout and paste that into your journal. Or you might choose to copy into your journal only certain significant passages from the letter.

Some people also incorporate into their journals letters they have received. In this way they keep a chronological record of the correspondence. You might also want to add your reactions to the letter, and your reply.

The journal can also be an aid to letter writing. When I sit down to write to a friend, I have only to look back on the past weeks or months in my journal to find plenty of thoughts and experiences to share. Then, instead of the spur-of-the-moment thoughts, I usually have something more substantive to write.

One friend who had been a missionary in India and Africa said that her journal consisted mainly of letters she wrote during that time.

> The "journal" I kept during my seven years in India and our ten years in Africa took the form of long letters to my mother, which she saved for me. There were limitations with these, of course. I didn't open up and unload all my troubles because I felt that would cause too much anxiety, especially with so many hundreds of miles separating us. But even with the limitations, those letters have some marvelous records for me. They tell me a great deal more than just what happened when.

There is another kind of letter that can go into your journal—the *unsent* letter that you write with no intention of mailing (see chapter 6). This gives you the benefit of working out some feelings and expressing them when a more direct confrontation would be impossible or unwise.

15. Travel

Some people begin a journal or maintain one especially when they are traveling. Instead of taking photos—or in addition to photos—they keep a written record of their trip, including as much detail as they have time to write. Back home, the traveler can relive the trip by means of the memories stored in the journal. Or one can make up a travel book consisting of snapshots, picture postcards, and other memorabilia together with one's journal entries. This makes an excellent family project, and is a good way to build family memories.

In his fascinating travel journal, *Voyage to the Far East,* theologian Helmut Thielicke explains how his journal keeping helped to intensify his experience of travel.

> Very soon after the trip began I had to write all kinds of notes in my diary to give some order to the often chaotic welter of impressions

I was experiencing and allow them to take intellectual shape. The writing of it went on quite apart from any literary designs, like a process of nature going on within me without any intervention of will and purpose. Sometimes, when the ship was rolling and pitching—or when the tropical heat made the paper stick fast to my arm, only to lose its sticky mooring in the next moment and fly away—actually I had no desire to write at all. Whenever that happened I had a feeling of emptiness, as if the voyage were not taking place at all: something like the process of reproduction was needed in order to allow these impressions to reach the conscious mind and become something more than dreamy meanderings.

The very act of writing made this voyage a far more intensive experience, and when I began to note this, gradually the joy of giving it structure came over me.[7]

16. Observations of nature

I keep a separate "green journal" in which I record observations of nature around our log cabin in the woods in northwest Wisconsin: sightings of animals and birds, wildflowers blooming in the woods, weather phenomena, and a record of gardening—planting, fertilizing, thinning, harvesting. I often refer back to these journals to remind myself of when I planted or when certain flowers were blooming or when I picked a specific vegetable, or when a killing frost signaled the end of a season.

I find entries like these:

March 8. This morning I saw a totally white furbearer emerge from a snowbank by the garage. It was about eighteen inches long, and had black eyes and small peaked ears. I think it was a long-tailed weasel.

March 24. At 7:00 A.M. only four degrees with the windchill below zero. The winter is getting too long! Where is global warming when we need it?

April 8. I took my first "spring" walk in our woods. All the low spots, which Hans refers to as "ephemeral wetlands," are filled with water. At the edge of the woods the first daffodils and crocus are sprouting.

April 11. Tonight the frogs came out in force—both sopranos and altos. Two pileated woodpeckers on the big maple.

May 6. I planted lettuce, radishes, and arugula in the afternoon, and in the evening it rained. The woodchuck made many trips, carrying paper and leaves down into her burrow (I'm assuming it's a female and that she's preparing a nursery).

You might ask: What does this have to do with a spiritual journal? In my view, spirituality has to do with all of life, not just some category labeled religion. And my spirituality includes a love of the creation and a commitment to care for the earth.

Even if you're a city dweller, you can become a "noticer" of the creation in your backyard, in a nearby park, or on short trips to the countryside. I recommend the beautiful book *Keeping a Nature Journal: Discovering a Whole New Way of Seeing the World around You* by Clare Walker Leslie and Charles E. Roth.

17. Other materials: drawings, clippings, photos

The contents of your journal need not be limited to handwritten or typed words. Some people with a flair for art (or just a penchant for doodling) like to include drawings. No art critic is present, and you don't have to compare yourself with Leonardo da Vinci or Rembrandt.

Others turn their journal into something like a scrapbook by pasting in newspaper clippings, magazine pictures, photos, or anything else that has personal meaning and can be attached to a page. It is also possible to attach a pocket to your journal into which you can slip clippings or pictures. If you're using a three-ring binder, you can add a plastic sleeve to hold these findings.

Experiment with your journal. Try adding some nonverbal materials and see what happens.

Now you have an idea of the kinds of observations and materials that can become valuable parts of your Daily Record. I hope your imagination has been expanded to see the possibilities for producing a creative journal—a unique record of your life and thoughts.

Beginning Your Daily Record

Following is a list of questions to help you get started in your Daily Record. Of course, you do not have to answer all of them. Some of them may be inappropriate, you may have nothing to say about them, or you may choose not to answer them. The questions are offered to jog your thinking. Answer in as few or as many words as you choose. The questions can be answered in the evening about the day just past, or in the morning about the previous day.

- As I look back on the day, what were the most significant events?
- In what ways was this day unique, different from other days?
- Did I have any particularly meaningful conversations?
- Did I do any reading? What were my reactions to it?
- How did I feel during the day? What were the emotional high points or low points? Why did I feel as I did? Is God trying to tell me anything through these feelings?
- Did I find myself worrying about anything today? Can I turn that worry into a prayer?
- What were the chief joys of the day? What did I accomplish?
- Did I fail at anything? What can I learn from this?
- What did I learn today? When did I feel most alive?

Those questions explore the day just past. You might also want to look ahead in your journal and answer questions like these.

- What do I hope to accomplish the rest of today (or tomorrow)?
- Are there any situations I will be facing that I should write a prayer about right now?

Chapter 5

Maintaining Momentum

If, after writing this far, you've begun keeping a journal, you are moving in the right direction. The purpose of this chapter is to help you gain momentum so that journal writing becomes a firmly established habit.

Toward that end I submit these basic principles of journal keeping.

1. Your way of keeping a journal is the right way

In my view, there is one cardinal rule about keeping a journal: *There are no rules for keeping a journal!* Your way is the right way.

I want to emphasize this because when you begin to keep a journal it is natural to wonder, "Am I doing this correctly?" "Is this the way a journal is supposed to sound?" "Is this good writing?" and so on. Some of us are more prone to that kind of self-doubt than others, but one of the great values of a journal is that you can write without being judged.

If you make journal writing a painstaking exercise in perfection, you probably will not keep it up for long. It will become too heavy a burden. So relax. Live by grace. Just write. No one is correcting your journal; no one is giving it a grade.

If you are particularly tempted to be perfectionistic about your journal, you might try what one friend does when he is uptight about making mistakes in his journal. He makes a *deliberate* mistake. He misspells a word or scribbles on the page or makes a grammatical error. Then, with that nice, white, perfect page spoiled, he feels free to write with ease. That may sound silly to you, but if you're so concerned with keeping a perfect journal that you are too inhibited to write in it, you might try this technique.

You might also find yourself wondering, "What would so-and-so think if he or she read this?" This important issue of privacy is covered in chapter 12, but for now I'll make this suggestion: Stop and write about this feeling. Explore it. Are you playing to an audience when you write in your journal? Is that a realistic audience? Why are you playing to that audience?

One friend tells how he overcame his fear of keeping a journal:

> From high school days on I had always wanted to keep a journal but thought it was unmanly, so I didn't. But when I went to college, a star athlete (lettered in several sports) shared with me the journal that he'd kept since tenth grade. That was enough for me. I bought a journal the next day and have kept one ever since.

2. Be honest

This leads directly to the second principle of journal writing. *Be honest.* Write how you really feel and not how you think you *should* feel. Record what you really think, not what you believe you *ought* to think.

Even if you feel you can't be honest with some people in other situations in life, for your own benefit be honest in your journal. No one else is looking, except God, who already knows the truth anyway.

We have no better examples of this kind of honesty than the Psalms, which is one reason this book is a favorite of mine. There is no pretense before God, no pious posturing—just openness and transparency.

We read words like these:

> *How long, O Lord? Will you forget me forever?*
> *How long will you hide your face from me?*
> *How long must I wrestle with my thoughts*
> *and every day have sorrow in my heart?*
> *How long will my enemy triumph over me?* (Ps. 13:1-2)

> *My God, my God, why have you forsaken me?*
> *Why are you so far from saving me,*
> *so far from the words of my groaning?*

O my God, I cry out by day, but you do not answer,
by night, and am not silent. (Ps. 22:1-2)

You know how I am scorned, disgraced, and shamed;
all my enemies are before you.
Scorn has broken my heart
and has left me helpless,
I looked for sympathy, but there was none,
for comforters, but I found none. (Ps. 69:19-20)

We can think of the Psalms as a form of journal writing—an honest-to-God reflection on critical situations in a believer's life. Later they were used in public worship, but like many of our great hymns, they grew out of a soul's honest encounter with God.

Think of Job and his honest cries to God. The Good News Bible reveals the almost shocking nature of Job's honesty:

You have worn me out, God;
you have let my family be killed.
You have seized me; you are my enemy.
I am skin and bones,
and people take that as proof of my guilt.
In anger God tears me limb from limb;
he glares at me with hate.
People sneer at me;
they crowd around me and slap my face.
God has handed me over to evil men.
I was living in peace,
but God took me by the throat
and battered me and crushed me.
God uses me for target practice
and shoots arrows at me from every side—
arrows that pierce and wound me; and even then he shows no pity.
He wounds me again and again;
he attacks like a soldier gone mad with hate. (Job 16:7-14, TEV)

What a model of religious honesty is "patient" Job!

So in your journal—if nowhere else—feel free to follow the example of the psalm writers and Job. Be honest with God. Wrestle with God, as Jacob did, until you are blessed.

3. Get at the feeling level

You can play it safe in your journal and stay at the level of outward events, restricting yourself to the facts of what happened. However, you get more benefit from journal writing if you include your feelings about what happened.

It is difficult to find a balanced approach to feelings in the Christian life. One can make too much of emotions and turn life into a frantic search for thrills. But we walk by faith, not emotions, and sometimes we must proceed by an act of will even against our feelings.

However, our feelings cannot be safely ignored, either. When we disregard feelings or suppress them, we ignore the fact that God created us as emotional, feeling people.

Our feelings can be symptoms, clues that something is wrong and needs to be reordered in our lives. Just as physical pain is a sign that something is wrong with our bodies, emotional pain can be a sign of something wrong in our spiritual-psychological systems.

So if you find yourself feeling fearful or anxious or depressed, explore that feeling in your journal. Express it in words. Write how you feel. Ask God to help you understand why you feel that way and what you can do about it.

When we write about our feelings in a journal, we are doing two things: (1) We diffuse the feelings by expressing them in a harmless way, and (2) we can begin to see them objectively and perhaps discern their causes and solutions.

One friend gives this advice: "Let your emotions get into your journal. Don't protect the page."

4. Experiment with your journal

I've already mentioned experimenting with the kind of notebook you use. Try different sizes, lined or unlined, fancy or plain, or use a

computer to word process your journal. It can make a difference in .
how you feel about writing.

Experiment also with the time at which you write. Try morning
or evening. Or try writing on and off through the day. See what feels
best.

Experiment with the place where you write. Maybe you will feel
more free to write outdoors, at a library, or on the front steps.

Try adding some of the kinds of material suggested in chapter 4,
including drawings, clippings, and photos. Let the journal become a
living organism, constantly in process.

Besides the Daily Record, try some of the exercises suggested in
Chapters 6-12.

One friend says: "Make your journal what *you* want it to be.
Others can give advice, but follow your own instincts in what you
want."

5. Don't take your journal too seriously

Journal writing should never become a grim chore. If you see it that
way, you probably will not do it for long. Writing in your journal is
not a task you must perform perfectly. Go at it in the spirit of creative
play. Think of your journal as a loyal friend. Let your journal-writing
time be a sabbath time for you, an enjoyable, quiet time, even a gift
you give yourself.

So relax with your journal, and enjoy it.

Chapter 6

Going Deeper

The exercises in this chapter are designed to foster spiritual growth in certain areas of your life. Some help with relationships, some with self-understanding, and some with life direction.

Read through them carefully. Some will seem more valuable to you than others. When you have extra time to write in your journal, work on one of these. Some of the techniques can be used more than once, in different ways—for example, unmailed letters and making lists.

Making Wise Decisions

One of my favorite Bible promises is James 1:5: "If any of you lacks wisdom, he should ask God, who gives generously to all without finding fault, and it will be given to him." God clearly promises to give us wisdom if we ask for it.

One of the ways you can open yourself to receive God's wisdom is by using your journal when you are faced with a decision.

In your journal, describe the decision you must make. Then make two columns: REASONS FOR and REASONS AGAINST. Jot down everything you can think of in both columns—even the most trivial concerns. If you have time, wait a day and come back to the list. You might want to add, change, or delete some items.

Ask God to give you wisdom and make the best decision you can on the basis of the two lists. Then ask yourself:

- Is this decision consistent with the word of God as I have learned it?
- Will this decision hurt me or anyone else, now or in the future?

- Is this decision consistent with my goals, my sense of where God is leading me?

It is always wise to discuss your decision with someone who is close to you. The Bible says, "Wisdom is found in those who take advice" (Prov. 13:10).

When you have done all these things, commit the decision to God and move ahead in faith.

In your journal, record the decision you made and the major reasons you decided that way.

Although this list making can be done outside a journal, there is value in having a record of your thinking. Later you may wonder why you decided as you did. By being able to review the reasons, you can be strengthened in your resolve—or learn how to make better decisions in the future.

Unmailed Letters

Have you ever "told someone off" in a letter and then, having released the pressure, destroyed the letter? It is a good method of catharsis, especially when we cannot confront the other person directly—either because we are not ready to do so or because we judge that the other person is not ready to receive what we say. Or the other person might be far away or might have died. Even if we are able to talk directly with the person, we may be able to do a better job after we have sorted out our thoughts in an unmailed letter.

The unmailed letter is not only to express anger or hurt. We might want to express our appreciation or love for a person but feel unable to do so directly.

I have known people who have worked out problems with deceased people by writing letters in their journals. In one case, a young woman had been alienated from her father, and the relationship was not healed before his death. She was able, in several letters to him, to write out feelings she had never been able to express directly. In this process she found peace and healing.

I used this method when one of my best friends died suddenly in Guadeloupe in the French West Indies. There was no way I could attend the funeral. I felt a need to mourn in some way, to find a way to say good-bye to my friend. I did this by writing him a long letter in my journal. By doing this I gained a sense of completeness, of closure, and felt at peace. (This is a journal entry I am not ready to share.)

You can also use the form of a letter as a way to pray, addressing the letter to God or to Jesus. No postage necessary!

Clarifying Your Beliefs

Beliefs are important because they influence how we feel and act. In our day, when there is so much confusion about ideas and morals, we need as much clarity about what we believe as possible. This is first of all for our own sakes, and then for the sake of our witness. In order to explain the Christian faith to others, we need to be clear on what we believe and why.

Attempting to put your beliefs into words is a great way to discover what you know or what you don't know. If you can't find the words, it is probably because you haven't thought things through.

Take any topic that is important to your beliefs:

God
Jesus Christ
The Holy Spirit
Prayer
Christian Life
The Bible

Begin by writing what you already believe. Try to do this in your own words. If you limit yourself to theological or religious clichés, you may simply be repeating words that have no real meaning for you. Often a test of understanding something is being able to put it into new words. If you can't say it another way, chances are you don't understand it yet.

A simple way to begin identifying your core beliefs, the ideas and principles by which you live, is to write your own creed. Write "I believe . . ." And then complete the sentence, stating some thought about life, human nature, God, your relationship with God. Don't worry about the order. Just begin. Then write another sentence, and another, until you feel you're finished for now. You can go back on succeeding days to add to the list or delete or revise the order.

Try to be honest to God. Write what you really do believe, so far as you can name it, rather than what someone else has said you ought to believe. I read once that teenagers in an adolescent treatment center were helped by writing one *true* sentence a day. As you write honestly about what you do believe, you will come to greater clarity and open your mind to receive new truths.

After listing what you believe "for sure," add what you are doubtful about and what you would like to know more about. Be honest here. There is no virtue in pretending to believe something you really are not sure about. Ask God to lead you to the books and people you need to answer your questions and to clarify your understanding.

As Others See Us

"O wud some power the giftie gie us! To see oursels as ithers see us." So wrote the Scottish poet Robert Burns. This suggests another interesting journal exercise that can give us new insights into ourselves.

Try writing about yourself in the third person ("He was . . ." "He did . . ." "She lived in . . ." "Her family was . . ."). Imagine you are a neutral observer. Write about your own present or your past. By writing as though you were an outsider, you may gain some objectivity you otherwise would not have.

Write your own eulogy. Project yourself into your imagined or idealized future. What would the eulogist say at your funeral? What would you want her to say?

Now imagine a hostile person—your worst enemy—writing about you. What would he say about you, about your strengths and weaknesses? Would there be truth in what he said?

How would some of the other key figures in your life—your father, your mother, your spouse, your children, a friend, a colleague—write about you?

Each of these exercises gives you some practice in stepping outside yourself, gaining an altered perspective on yourself.

Identifying Gifts

The Bible teaches clearly that all God's children are gifted.

> *There are varieties of gifts, but the same Spirit; and there are varieties of services, but the same Lord; and there are varieties of activities, but it is the same God who activates all of them in everyone. To each is given the manifestation of the Spirit for the common good* (1 Cor. 12:4-7, NRSV).

> *Each one should use whatever gift he has received to serve others, faithfully administering God's grace in its various forms* (1 Pet. 4:10).

This same idea of giftedness is also taught in the parable of the talents (Matt. 25:14-30). The giver is the same; the number of talents given differs. But each one is responsible to nurture these gifts and to use them for the welfare of the human family.

The gifts God has given us can be major clues as to what God wants us to do with our lives. Elizabeth O'Connor says it well:

> We ask to know the will of God without guessing that his will is written into our very beings. We perceive that will when we discern our gifts. Our obedience and surrender to God are in a large part our obedience and surrender to our gifts. This is the message wrapped up in the parable of the talents. Our gifts are all on loan. We are responsible for expending them in the world, and we will be held accountable.[1]

The missionary doctor Albert Schweitzer wrote, "At that point in life where your talent meets the needs of the world, that is where God wants you to be."

So a first step in becoming more clear about God's will for your life is to discern your gifts. Explore questions like this in your journal:

- What do you perceive your gifts to be?
- If you were to die today, which of your accomplishments would you feel best about?
- What kind of work gives you the most joy or satisfaction?
- What are the needs you see in your family, your church, your community, your world?
- Where do your gifts connect with these needs?

Making Lists

A very simple but powerful exercise that I use over and over again in my journal is list making. The utility of the practice is related to its simplicity. It generates ideas quickly and with little effort; it is not intimidating, so I find it easy to do.

Here's an example of list making. Write at the top of the page: "Fifty Things That Are Going Right in My Life." Down the side of the page write the numbers from 1 to 50. When you're ready to begin, just start listing whatever you can think of that is going well in your life. Do this in flow-writing fashion, jotting ideas as fast as you can without deliberating too much. Just let the ideas flow. If an idea comes up more than once, list it again. Keep going until you're done—or even go beyond 50. Then read back over the list and write an entry about what you observe.

In succeeding chapters of this book, you will find ways to use list making in connection with prayer, in looking backward at your life journey, in looking forward to gain a new vision for your future, in seeking healing and wholeness. And as you continue journaling, you will probably discover your own ways of using this fascinating method that often yields surprising insights.

You now are acquainted with the heart of the journal—the Daily Record—and you have learned many techniques to enrich and extend your journal. You are well along the journal road. The next chapter shows you how to use the journal to care for your soul.

Chapter 7

Caring for Your Soul

Swiss physician Paul Tournier writes: "The busier we are, the more do we become burdened with responsibilities, and the more do we stand in need of these times when we can renew our contact with God."[1]

As we look into the lives of many great Christians, we invariably find them mentioning the value of solitude, of a quiet time, a time of prayer and spiritual reading that enabled them to care for their own soul and to find strength and direction to do great things for God.

For a year I met once a month with a spiritual director who offered guidance in the practices that would strengthen my life with God. Together we decided that what I needed to care for my soul was some reading, some writing, and some prayer each day. The exact way I would do each of these would vary, but these were the essential practices to undergird my spiritual life.

As I worked on this, I found that my journal became the center for the other two practices of spiritual reading and prayer, a place to focus my thoughts, a place to record insights from the reading, a place to pray.

In this chapter, I'd like to suggest how you can use a journal in connection with spiritual reading and prayer as a way to care for your soul, your inner life.

Spiritual Reading
Meditating on Scripture
Some people question whether meditation has a place within Christian spirituality. Yet there is a long tradition of Christian meditation, and it is a good biblical word. The Psalms are especially rich in encouragements to meditate.

My eyes stay open through the watches of the night,
that I may meditate on your promises. (Ps. 119:148)

One generation will commend your works to another;
they will tell of your mighty acts.
They will speak of the glorious splendor of your majesty,
and I will meditate on your wonderful works. (Ps. 145:4-5)

I remember the days of long ago;
I meditate on all your works
and consider what your hands have done. (Ps. 143:5)

Psalm 1:2 praises those who "meditate day and night" on God's law.

When God gave marching orders to Joshua, he commanded, "Do not let this Book of the Law depart from your mouth; meditate on it day and night, so that you may be careful to do everything written in it. Then you will be prosperous and successful" (Josh. 1:8).

Although the New Testament does not use the word "meditate," the idea is certainly contained in passages like Philippians 4:8: "Finally, beloved, whatever is true, whatever is honorable, whatever is just, whatever is pure, whatever is pleasing, whatever is commendable, if there is any excellence and if there is anything worthy of praise, *think* about these things" (NRSV, emphasis added).

It is obvious from passages like these that meditation in the scriptural sense is not lazy, dreamy inactivity. Christian meditation is an active reflection on specific content. Most methods of Christian meditation are basically meditation on the Bible. Dietrich Bonhoeffer required a period of meditation for the students in his underground seminary in Nazi Germany. He declared:

> The Word of Scripture should never stop sounding in your ears and working in you all day long, just like the words of someone you love. And just as you do not analyze the words of someone you love, but accept them as they are said to you, accept the Word of Scripture and ponder it in your heart, as Mary did. That is all. That is meditation.

Do not look for new thoughts and connections in the text, as you would if you were preaching. Do not ask, "How shall I pass this on?" but, "What does it say to me?" Then ponder that Word long in your heart until it has gone right into you and taken possession of you.[2]

"Until it has gone right into you and taken possession of you." These words suggest the difference between meditation on the Word and reading or studying it. In reading or study we are engaged in an intellectual exercise; the emphasis is on learning new content. But in meditation we are seeking to internalize what we already know, letting it seep deeply down into the center of our beings where it can do its work.

The goal of meditation, then, is not to gain more intellectual knowledge, but to *experience* the truth at the deepest level of our beings. The aim is to gain a personal knowledge of God, which in turn will result in personal transformation. Dwight L. Moody said, "The Scriptures were not given to increase our knowledge, but to change our lives."

Andrew Murray put it this way:

God's Word only works its true blessing when the truth it brings to us has stirred the inner life, and reproduced itself in resolve, trust, love, or adoration. When the heart has received the Word through the mind and has had its spiritual powers called out and exercised on it, the Word is no longer void, but it has done that whereunto God has sent it. It has become part of our life, and strengthened us for new purpose and effort.[3]

There are many ways to meditate on Scripture. Here is one process:

1. Choose some portion of the Bible to read. It should probably be an entire book, because that respects the integrity of the Bible, the way it was written. Plan on staying with a book until you're through it; resist the temptation to skip around. If you are new at Bible reading, you may want to begin with the Psalms, one of the four Gospels, or one of the shorter epistles of Paul.

2. It may be helpful to read an introduction to the book or some commentary notes first.

3. When you come to the time of reading, take a few minutes to settle down, become comfortable, and relax, perhaps by concentrating on your breathing. Then ask God to bless your reading. You can do this in your own words or with the words of the young Samuel: "Speak, LORD, for your servant is listening" (1 Samuel 3:9).

4. Begin reading slowly and stop when a word or phrase seems highlighted for you, when it "shimmers" with meaning, when the Holy Spirit is addressing you through these words.

5. Reflect on the meaning of these words. Ask God for insight into the message you are receiving through this word.

Write down in your journal the thoughts that come to you. You will find the journal a helpful aid to concentration. There is something *generative* about the act of writing; thoughts will come to you while you write. After you have written your insights and questions, you will have a record of your spiritual growth. You can review this record and use it as a springboard for further growth.

While meditating on Jesus' words, "The Father is greater than I" (John 14:28), a pastor wrote these words in his journal:

> To have a sense of leisure I need to appreciate the truth that the Father is greater than I. As soon as I accept this reality, it permits me to float in the presence of God. To come to this sense of floating in the presence of God, I need a large space of time, not always finding myself at the edge of an entry or exit. A feeling of hurry gives me only a narrow glimpse of God, indeed reduces the largeness of God. When I tarry in the presence of God, I begin to appreciate his largeness.
>
> How tragic to become so important to the affairs of life that I become greater than the Father. I no longer have the space in which to be free. We need to step back from the rush of life and exclaim like Jesus, "The Father is greater than I." Leisure brings freedom, worship, identity, bliss. Jesus allowed time for solitude in his ministry. I need to do the same.

6. Pray. Speak to God about this. It might be a prayer of confession as you reflect on how your life falls short of this word. Or it might be a prayer of gratitude for a particular blessing, or a petition of help for yourself or someone else.

In your journal, record the words that especially spoke to you, together with your prayer. Don't worry whether the prayer sounds literary or well-written. Let it be an honest expression of your heart.

A friend wrote this prayer in her journal:

"Love is kind" (1 Cor. 13:4)
Lord, often I am not kind.
I am blunt and direct
and speak
without stopping to think
how my words will affect
the one to whom I am speaking.
If only, if only,
I could take the time
to slip out of myself,
to abandon my viewpoint
and move over into the other person's position,
how different my speech would be.
Some things would go unsaid.
Instead I would learn to trust God to work things out.
Instead of opening my big mouth
and feeling that if I don't set things right
things won't be corrected,
I would listen.
How often have I trodden over sensitive hearts
with words and tone
that could be likened to
heavy cobble-soled army boots.
Lord, help me to temper
honesty and directness
with kindness.

7. Be still for a few moments in God's presence. Listen to what God is saying; be aware of the presence of God's Spirit within you.

In this process of holy reading, you may read only one verse or a few verses. You might read a whole chapter before you find something that especially speaks to you. Your aim is not speed reading or reading a set amount. You are listening for God's word to you.

There are a few things to remember about this process of meditating on Scripture. You do not have to be in some special mood to do this. It's important to keep at it regularly, despite your feelings or your apparent lack of success. George Macdonald wrote:

> That man is perfect in faith who can come to God in the utter dearth of his feelings and desires, without a glow or an aspiration, with the weight of low thoughts, failures, neglects, and wandering forgetfulness, and say to him, "Thou art my refuge."[4]

Don't be bothered too much by distractions. If while you are pondering a passage of Scripture your thoughts wander to some situation or person, pray briefly and commit that situation to God. Then allow your thoughts to return to the passage.

Don't be frustrated if your meditation on Scripture does not yield instant results in your life. This process involves the slow making over of your thinking and emotions, and that takes time. But to those who remain faithful to the discipline, results will come. A.W. Tozer describes this process:

> I think for the average person the progression will be something like this: First, a sounding as of a presence walking in the garden. Then a voice, more intelligible, but still far from clear. Then the happy moment when the Spirit begins to illuminate the Scriptures, and that which had been only a sound, or at best a voice, now becomes an intelligible word, warm and intimate and clear as the word of a dear friend. Then will come life and light, and best of all, ability to see and rest in and embrace Jesus Christ as Savior and Lord and All.[5]

Paraphrasing the Scriptures

Another way to use your journal as an aid to your devotional life is to paraphrase or rewrite a selected portion of Scripture in your own words. Doing this forces you to come to grips with the meaning of the words and their application to your life.

The Psalms are supreme examples of prayer, and they are especially good for this exercise. They express many moods of the spiritual life. However, the imagery often is not part of our lives today, especially if we live in an urban setting. For example, phrases about "sheep and shepherds" may mean more to you if you restate them in other words. City children were asked to paraphrase Psalm 23, beginning with "The Lord is my Shepherd." One teen-age boy wrote, "The Lord is my parole officer." To him, this was the person who best exemplified God's love and care.

Here is my paraphrase of Psalm 63:

Oh God, my God,
I am searching for you with my whole self.
My spirit thirsts for your Spirit
like a man lost in a parching desert.
There have been times in the past
when I experienced your strengthening power as I prayed in the
silence of a cathedral or worshiped in a country church.
Now I will continue to praise you
because your love means more to me than life itself.
I know that you will once again fill my life with meaning.
As I lie awake in the middle of the night,
I will remember you, O God.
I can relax and trust you
because you are always my help.
All the forces
within me and outside
that try to pull me down
will be defeated.
I will again praise the Lord
who gives me joy.

Oswald Chambers wrote, "To re-write the Psalms into a free language of expression of one's own has proved to me a valuable treasurehouse of self-expression to God."

In a Bible class on Romans, each of us had to create our own paraphrase, trying to state as accurately as we could our understanding of this major statement of Christian doctrine. The same process would work well with the other Epistles or the Gospels.

When you paraphrase portions of the Bible, what you write probably will not match the poetic grandeur of the original. It may not even be absolutely accurate in the scholarly sense. But it will be your own understanding of the Bible. In the process of recasting the words, you will be internalizing the Word and making it your own.

Reflecting on a Spiritual Classic

The same process we used in meditating on Scripture can be used to dialog with spiritual classics. By spiritual classics I mean great books in which Christian thinkers have shared their wisdom about the Christian life, especially the life of prayer and the inner life with God. These classics are often densely packed with wisdom, and are best read in short sections, pondering their meaning and applying it to our own lives as we do in meditating on the Bible.

Here are some of the best-loved classics that deserve careful reading:

Brother Lawrence, *The Practice of the Presence of God*
Augustine, *Confessions*
Thomas à Kempis, *The Imitation of Christ*
Thomas Kelly, *Testament of Devotion*
Evelyn Underhill, *School of Charity*
Francois Fenelon, *Christian Perfection*
St. Francis de Sales, *Introduction to the Devout Life*

Why read the classics—these books written in a different time, in a different culture from ours? These books have stood the test of time. By reading a selection of them we receive wisdom from the whole Christian church, rather than only our own tradition. In the classics we may find ideas not present to us in contemporary books. C.S. Lewis, in his excellent essay "On Reading Old Books," says:

> "Every age has its own outlook. It is specially good at seeing certain truths and specially liable to make certain mistakes. We all, therefore, need the books that will correct the characteristic mistakes of our own period." For this reason, Lewis encourages us to read one old book for every new one to "keep the clean sea breeze of the centuries blowing through our minds."[6]

As you explore these spiritual classics, you will find those that especially speak to you. They will then be worth many successive readings. In order to find your way to those classics that will become your own special books, you might try these samplers:

Paul Ofstedal, ed. *These Words upon Your Heart: Daily Reflections on Spiritual Classics*. This book contains selections from twelve classic writers with reflections by contemporary Christians.

Richard J. Foster and James Bryan Smith, eds. *Devotional Classics*. In addition to fifty-two selected readings, this book includes reflection questions and spiritual exercises.

One procedure I have followed in dialoging with these classics is to read until I find a passage that especially speaks to me. I copy that passage into my journal and jot down any thoughts I have about it and why it has special meaning for me. Then I turn it into a prayer. Praying about our spiritual reading keeps it from being merely an intellectual exercise; it engages our emotions and our wills.

Here is an example from my reading of *The Imitation of Christ*.

> "If you can be quiet and suffer for a while, you will, without doubt, see the help of God come in your need. He knows the time and the place to deliver you, and therefore you must resign yourself wholly to him. It is God's concern to deliver from all confusion" (*Imitation*, p. 29).

Lord, in my present problem,
help me to believe these words.
Give me the patience to bear what
must be borne in this situation.
Enable me to wait for your help.
In your own time give me what is
right for me and helpful to others.

Someone has distinguished between reading for our *information* and reading for our *formation*. This reading of the spiritual classics is certainly for our formation. Therefore, the quantity of our reading is not as important as the quality. We are not reading so much for intellectual growth as to open ourselves to the Spirit's transforming power.

Remember, the act of writing will help you focus your thoughts and will encourage creativity, enabling you to have thoughts you otherwise would not have. If you keep a written record of your dialog in your journal, you can review these key ideas and deepen their impression.

By bringing something new into our minds and hearts, spiritual reading gets us beyond our own ruminations. It is a way of listening to God. In *Learning and Teaching Christian Meditation*, Avery Brooke says:

> Meditation, when understood as listening prayer, is our primary means of getting to know God. When, for instance, we meditate on the Bible, we are not merely reading an ancient text. We are listening to God through the text. Sometimes what we hear is the merest whisper from God and sometimes it is a sudden and unexpected insight. Always it is personal. God is not just relating to the people of the Bible, but to us. We respond to what we hear, and we are in a living relationship with God.[7]

Methodist bishop Lance Webb writes about what he calls his "living-the-faith notebooks."

> I began, what has been for me, one of the most helpful disciplines in my entire life. In a book with a blank page for every day in the

year, I wrote down the selections from the Scripture, the experience of some other seeker of truth, a poem, the verse of a hymn, or the honest description of what was taking place within me.

Generally, I would read until I came upon a sentence or a paragraph that really spoke to me. I recorded the selection in my own poor handwriting (which most people can't read), and then I wrote my appropriate response. Sometimes it was a confession. At other times there were insights into why I failed and decisions as to what I was to do about the situation I was facing. Often it was to write my new commitment, my new trust, and my thanksgiving and praise for the one in whose presence I can truthfully say, "I have strength for anything through him who gives me power."[8]

Prayer

The preceding activities have all been exercises in listening, receiving, absorbing, and hearing God speak to you. Your journal can also be a place where you speak to God by recording your prayers.

As with the other activities, writing out your prayers is an aid to concentration, helping you cope with wandering thoughts, especially when you are tired or particularly busy.

Some people like to date the prayers, and then later record when and how God answered. This is not a way of keeping score of God; it is a method of strengthening one's faith.

In writing your prayers, do not worry about creating a spiritual or literary masterpiece. Just express yourself in your own words.

A friend, in her seventies, wrote this in her journal:

Lord, your word tells us that the righteous are planted in the house of the Lord; they flourish in your courts. They bring forth fruit in old age. They are ever full of sap and green (Ps. 92).

Lord, fill me with your Spirit; help me bring forth fruit in my old age. I sing your praises for you are my rock, my sure foundation. Praise your holy name. Help me to truly worship you today.

In whatever situation I am in today may I so respond that your name will be glorified.

I'd like to add a few simple forms of "writing prayer" that I use regularly. Some of these involve journaling exercises introduced earlier in this book.

Please/Thank You Prayers

This simple form of prayer makes use of the list-making technique described in chapter 6. This way of praying is so simple and easy that I do it every day. It's based on some of the first words we teach our children: *please* and *thank you.*

I begin with *thank you* as a way of reminding myself of the blessings that have come to me. In my journal I write the heading: "Today I give thanks to the Lord of Life especially:" Then I simply list what comes to mind. I have listed blessings like these:

1. For safe driving to Iowa City and back.
2. For all the help Paul is receiving.
3. For good slow rain, so needed by the garden.
5. That I was able to finish a chapter of *How to Keep a Spiritual Journal.*

I then turn to *please,* praying for myself and others. I ask myself, "Who needs my prayers today?" I write the heading: "Today I pray the Lord of Life especially:" And I move on to making my list.

1. For Bob: that he is led to his right work, his right place, his right people.
2. For Paul: healing of body, mind, and spirit.
3. For myself: that I am led to the books and ideas I need to revise my book on journaling.
4. For Rebecca: safe travel in Mexico and Kansas City.
5. For Jeff and Debbie: a new vision of a good life for them.

Letters to God

Try writing letters to God or Jesus or the Holy Spirit. (See "Unmailed Letters" in chapter 6.) In the Bible and Christian tradition, God has many names. Experiment with using varieties of them and see how it affects your prayer.

You may find the form of a letter liberating, freeing you from the need to write in a specialized theological or spiritual vocabulary.

You may take another step and use your sanctified imagination to write what you think God is saying to you by return mail.

Listening Prayer

What are the questions you are living? Write them in your journal. Ask God to lead you to the ideas and insights you need. Write what comes to you at the moment. Stay alert and watch for answers that come from your reading, from sermons, conversations, radio, or TV. God has many channels through which truth can reach you!

I don't presume that everything that comes into my mind is from God. It takes discernment to identify what is truly from God, and the journal is a good place to undertake that, as we reflect on what we've written, compare it with what we know from other sources—the Bible, subsequent Christian literature, conversations with friends and loved ones.

Praying for Others

Prayer involves more than just asking for things for ourselves. An important element of prayer is intercession—our prayers for others. We should pray first for those people and causes that are closest to us. Charles F. Whiston writes:

> We should have a definite list of those for whom we intercede. It is better to pray daily for a few than only infrequently for many. It is God himself who gives us those for whom we are to intercede. A special part of his universe he entrusts to our care, and for that part we are to pray.[9]

One way we can do this is to distribute our concerns over the days of the week. Reserve a page in your journal and list the days of the week. For each day write the names of those people or causes you want to remember in prayer. It might be appropriate to pray for those in your local church on Sunday, for your place of employment on Monday, and so on.

For a longer intercession list, you could number a page with the days of the month and then assign people and concerns to this list.

Without such a list or system, it is hard to carry out systematic and regular intercession—an important part of our Christian service.

Pray the Plotted Day

This can be done in the evening, praying for the day to come, or in the morning as you look forward to the day. Let your mind move through the day from beginning to end, as far as you can see it, and pray about the work you have to do, the people you will be with, the meetings, the travel, the pleasures you expect to enjoy. Ask God's blessings for each one.

Findings

To enrich your own prayers, copy into your journal prayers you find in books, magazines, church bulletins, on the Internet, or in other unexpected places. See the bibliography for some recommended prayer anthologies.

To motivate and guide your prayer life, copy into your journal Bible passages and other quotations about prayer that especially strike you and that you want to be able to call up.

I copied into my journal this quote from C. S. Lewis: "The prayer preceding all prayers is, 'May it be the real I who speaks. May it be the real thou that I speak to.'"[10]

We learn to pray by praying, and as you use your journal for prayer, you will discover your own ways, changing over time, of writing prayer.

Chapter 8

Looking Backward

The Bible is rich in encouragements to "remember."

Remember the former things, those of long ago (Is. 46:9).

Remember the wonders he has done, his miracles, and the judgments he pronounced (1 Chr. 16:12).

Remember those earlier days after you had received the light, when you stood your ground in a great contest in the face of suffering (Heb. 10:32).

Remember the words I spoke to you (John 15:20).

Remember your leaders, who spoke the word of God to you. Consider the outcome of their way of life and imitate their faith (Heb. 13:7).

When you remember, you relive and reclaim your own past. You can tell where you are on the journey of life only by seeing where you have been.

Mark Scannell, a teacher of journaling, writes:

Remembering is not nostalgically recalling the good old days; rather, it takes place in terms of an interplay between where I am in the present and where I move in my past. It is a retelling of the stories of my life in terms of what is taking place now. Through remembering, I begin to work with experiences from the past which can teach me concerning my present situation or enable me to bring closure to past events still unfinished. Remembering enables one to move with the energy which is contained within the past experience of life; it frees and unlocks energy which has been locked up in past experiences. This working with the past in terms of the present also has the possibility of moving us into our future with power and energy. Moving into the past enables us to move into the future. Remembering in this way we can also bring about the healing of past experiences which continue to be painful and hurting. The present working can strengthen us to a point where it becomes possible to face and work with these past painful and disconnecting experiences.[1]

Remembering is not a morbid preoccupation with former sins or difficult situations. (There is a holy forgetfulness!) Some memories may be too painful to be dredged up at the present time, and might be better left untouched. At the same time, trying to bury the past forever is also dangerous. Eventually we have to look back in order to be healed completely.

Alvin Toffler coined the term "future shock" to describe the feeling of "dis-ease" we experience when we face too much change in too short a time. We are a people on the move, often without roots. One way we can gain a cushion against future shock is by being rooted in our own history.

As mentioned in chapter 4, some event or something you read may spontaneously trigger a memory. But now we are going to look at several ways you can explore your past in a more systematic and comprehensive fashion.

Read through the exercises and see which ones seem most interesting or valuable to you. Then, when you have additional time to write in your journal, do one or more of these "Looking Backward" exercises.

The Chapters of Your Life

Imagine that you are writing your autobiography. How would your life divide into chapters? Begin with your birth and look for the next major division point. Maybe it is a move, the birth of a brother or sister, or perhaps starting school. Then continue dividing your life into chapters on the basis of where you lived, what you did, and what was going on in your life.

The chapters in my Life Book follow a pattern of school and work. (Yours might look much different.)

- Birth and Preschool Years
- Elementary School
- High School
- College
- First Teaching Job
- Graduate School and College Teaching
- Working at Concordia Publishing House
- Book Editor at Augsburg Publishing House
- Missionary Service in Madagascar
- Freelance Writing and Editing
- Director, Augsburg Books
- Life at the Homestead

Try to determine the chapters of your life. Your pattern may be much different from mine, perhaps focusing more on relationships or inner events.

If you want to expand your imagination, you could try to add some chapters, imagining the future as you want it to be.

Once you have discovered the basic pattern of your life, you might want to write under each of the chapter headings some of the most important events, people, or experiences that happened in that period of your life.

I have found it helpful to reenter a chapter of my life with these questions:

- What was life-enhancing during this period? What enriched my life? What made it more interesting, pleasant, or productive?
- Who or what did I love at this time?
- Who were the people I was closest to in this chapter?

In answering these questions, you can simply make a list, or you can write in more detail about some or all of the subjects.

Your Life Story

A friend of mine says that we all owe it to our children and grand-children to write our autobiography. He himself has written his life story, and I'm at work on mine, at this point titled *An Unfinished Life*. Unless you have a very unusual story or are famous or write with great literary flare, you probably will not have publishers knocking at your door with a contract to publish your book. But with today's print technology, you can easily share your life story with those who mean the most to you.

This exercise contains a series of questions to help you explore your past.[2] Of course, not all the categories or questions will fit for you; you need not answer them all. Answer those that seem most interesting and helpful.

You might want to start with your earliest memories and move chronologically through your life. Or you could work in reverse, start-ing with the freshest memories and working backwards.

Another approach is to begin with the time or chapter of your life that you feel you most want to work through. This might be a time of crisis or uncertainty, or it could be a particularly joyful time.

A. Childhood
- What are your earliest memories?
- In your preschool years did you have any religious experiences you can remember?
- What are your happiest memories of this time?
- Were there any stressful events?

B. Elementary-School Life
- Where did you live?
- How did this environment influence you?
- Who were the people to whom you felt closest?
- What good times did you experience?
- Do you have any painful memories from this time?
- How did you feel about school?
- What kind of reading did you do during these years?

- Did you have any family responsibilities?
- Did your religious life change during this period?

C. Junior-High and High-School Years
- Who were your closest friends during these years?
- How did they influence you?
- How was your relationship with your parents?
- How did you feel about yourself during this period?
- Which teachers influenced you most?
- Did you develop special interests or take part in extracurricular activities?
- What were your most difficult struggles during this period?
- What were your first sexual experiences and how did you feel about them?
- Did your spiritual life change in any significant ways?
- What work experiences did you have?
- What were your main accomplishments during these years?

D. College
- Why did you go to college?
- Why did you choose the college that you did?
- Who were your most influential teachers?
- Did you become involved in any social or political issues?
- Who were the friends who influenced you most?
- What were your activities, besides studying?
- What happened to your religious beliefs during this time?
- What was your major and why did you choose it?
- How would you describe your social life at this time?
- Did you finish college? If not, why not?

E. Work Experience
- What was your first full-time job?
- How did you react to it?
- What jobs have you held since then?
- What were the biggest problems you faced in your work?

- What experience have you gained through this work?
- Do you have any mentor or model in your work?
- In what direction is your work taking you?

F. Courtship and Marriage
- How did you meet your spouse?
- What were your first impressions of him or her?
- Why did you choose this person as a spouse?
- How long after you met did you start making marriage plans?
- Describe your wedding.
- Where was your first home or apartment?
- How did marriage affect your spiritual life?
- How were you accepted by your in-laws?
- What were the biggest adjustments in your marriage?
- Has the marriage ended? If so, how?

G. *Raising a Family*
- List the names and birth dates of your children.
- What are the strengths, weaknesses, and special interests of each one?
- What has been your relationship with each child?
- How have you tried to pass your religious faith on to them?
- What have been your most enjoyable family times?
- What problems or challenges have you faced as a family?

H. *Settling In*
- Did you change your business or work?
- Were you active in a political party?
- In what ways did you contribute to the life of your church?
- Which friends were most important to you at this time?
- Did you change your place of residence?
- How would you describe your relationship to God at this time?
- What did you do for recreation?
- What were your major goals?
- Did you do any traveling during this period?

I. Retirement Years
- In what ways did you plan for retirement?
- How did you feel about retiring?
- What do you see as the major achievements of your life?
- What goals still lie ahead of you?
- What lessons have you learned through living?
- Who are the most important people in your life now?
- What causes or institutions have you championed? Would you do it again?
- How do you view the prospect of your death?
- Make an imaginary will in which you bequeath your personal possessions to family and friends.
- At this point in your life, what are your thoughts about God?

A check at a library or bookstore or on the Internet will lead you to many fine books to help you tell your life story. Two of my favorites are *Writing the Memoir: From Truth to Art* by Judith Barrington, and *Your Life As Story: Writing the New Autobiography* by Tristine Rainer.

Your Spiritual Journey

The Old Testament is the story of God's relationship with a people, the children of Israel. It is a pattern of call and response, closeness and rebellion.

In the same way, each of us has a history of our relationship with God that fluctuates between nearness and distance, connection and disconnection, communion and resistance. It is helpful to remember history—both the high points and the low points—and to learn from it.

Think back over your life, perhaps in "The Chapters of Your Life." What were the religious experiences of each period of your life? When did you feel closest to God? When did you feel you were farthest from the Divine Presence?

You might even want to chart the highs and lows on a graph, giving a visual sense of your spiritual journey.

When you have finished writing about your spiritual journey, or when you have graphed it, reflect on what you see there.

- Are there any lessons you can learn from the journey?
- Are there any patterns?
- What can you learn from this that will influence your future spiritual growth?

Here are some additional exercises to help you explore your spiritual journey.

Spiritual Mentors

List the five people who have most influenced your faith. (Of course, you can list more than five.) Jot down what each one did to influence your spiritual development. Choose one to write about in more detail. Consider writing a letter to one or more of your spiritual mentors, expressing your gratitude. This could be an unmailed letter (See chapter 6), or you could mail it if that's possible.

Pilgrimages

In the Middle Ages, pilgrims visited places associated with the Christian faith. In your journal, list the places that have been especially significant for your faith journey—homes, churches, schools, a camp, a retreat center, a setting in nature. In a brief entry describe each place and tell what happened there to influence your spiritual growth. Choose one or more to write up in greater detail.

People of the Book

What was your relationship with the Bible in each decade of your life (0-9, 10-19, 20-29, etc.)? How were you learning from it? Who were your favorite people in the Bible? What were your favorite Bible stories or passages? Was there any time when your relationship with the Bible was strained? What happened? Where is the relationship today? Where would you like it to be in the future?

Gratitude Journal

Do a list-making exercise (see chapter 6), using the heading: "Fifty Things I'm Glad I Did in Life."

On Trial

Imagine that you are on trial for being a Christian. As you stand in the dock, what is the evidence brought against you?

For additional ways to explore your spiritual journey, see *Remembering Your Story: A Guide to Spiritual Autobiography* (Upper Room, 1996) by Richard L. Morgan.

James C. Fenhagen summarizes the value of grasping the shape of our spiritual journey:

> A God-seeker is a person on a journey. When the thirst has been awakened, we are no longer persons wandering aimlessly about, but rather persons who have begun to discern the bare outlines of a path. We become more than wanderers. We are people seeking for those signs that will point us in the direction that will allow our journey to unfold.[3]

Chapter 9

Looking Forward

One of the things I find fascinating and beneficial about a journal is the way it allows me to move through three dimensions of time—present, past, and future. By enabling me to live with greater awareness, my journal helps me live more fully, more intentionally, in the present. Drawing on memory, journal writing assists me in exploring my own past, seeing patterns, becoming more conscious of the flow of my life. In the journal I can also envision my desired future, clarify my life purposes, establish goals, and advance toward them.

Envisioning Your Future

Through the prophet Jeremiah, God gave this promise: "For surely I know the plans I have for you, says the Lord, plans for your welfare and not for harm, to give you a future with hope" (Jer. 29:11, NRSV). And the psalm writer prayed, "May [God] grant your heart's desire and fulfill all your plans" (Ps. 20:4, NRSV).

Here are a few journal-writing exercises to free your imagination to envision a future guided by hope and desire.

Before I Die

Using the list-making technique introduced in chapter 6, write about "One Hundred Things I Want to Do Before I Die." Let your imagination run free. Allow yourself to repeat some items. Postpone the question, "Do I *really* want to do this?" and don't worry about the practicality of some of your desires. It's important to identify the desires and hopes that give you reason to live. When you finish your list, read back over it and write a journal entry or a letter to God about your hopes and plans.

I Have a Dream

Dr. Martin Luther King, Jr., gave a famous speech in which he declared, "I have a dream . . ." What are your dreams for the future—for yourself, your family, the human family? Allow yourself to dream with hope. At this point don't be concerned with how realistic or practical your dreams are. Consider the kind of world you would like to see. Complete these sentences:

I have a dream . . .

I have a dream . . .

I have a dream . . .

Your dream is already a prayer.

Back from the Future

In your imagination move forward twenty-five years from now. Imagine that the twenty-five years that have just gone by are the best years of your life—the happiest, most blessed, most fruitful. Describe what has happened in that quarter-century.

Write a letter from the person you are then to the person you are now.

Dying and Rising

The pattern for the Christian life was set by Jesus in his death and resurrection. Martin Luther, following St. Paul, saw the Christian life as a daily death and rebirth—as the old nature dies and the new nature lives in God's resurrection power.

Look for this pattern in your life. What is dying in your life (relationships, commitments, dreams, goals)? What is rising? Where are the signs of greening?

Spiritual Legacy

I'm haunted by the country-western song with the repeated refrain, "What will I leave behind?" Imagine that you have reached the end of your pilgrimage on earth.

In your mind, pass through the rooms of your house. What objects identify you as a Christian or symbolize your faith (art objects, books, jewelry, CDs)? List them and then after each object write the name of the person to whom you would like to bequeath this treasure as a way of demonstrating the importance of Christian faith in your life.

Then think of nonmaterial spiritual resources you would like to pass on. For example:

My knowledge of the Bible I bequeath to . . .

My joy in singing in the choir I bequeath to . . .

My concern to feed the hungry I pass on to . . .

Look back over this entry. Does it offer any insights into actions you should be taking right now?

The Final Journey

Take fifteen minutes to write what you believe about death and life after death. Where did these ideas come from? What questions do you have?

Ask yourself: Has my life been wasted? What do I still need to do? If I knew I had six months to live, what would I do?

Write your own obituary. How do you want to be remembered?

Write a letter to God about this final journey.

Having done one or more of these visioning exercises, you can move on with new insights to clarify your life purposes.

Clarifying Major Life Purposes

Set aside an hour or more to think about your values, about what is most important to you. For example, how important to you are the following items?

- Having a good marriage and family life
- Owning a beautiful home
- Doing satisfying work
- Being able to travel widely
- Being physically fit and attractive
- Making a substantial salary
- Having many friends

- Growing spiritually
- Furthering your education
- Working for peace and justice in the world
- Being active in your church

Questions like these may also help you clarify what is important to you.

- If you were guaranteed a salary for the rest of your life, how would you spend your time?
- What changes would you most like to see in your life?
- If you knew you had only one year to live, what would you do with that time?

Questions like these can get us off the treadmill of unquestioning activity and give us some perspective as to what is most important for us.

In your journal, make a list of your major life purposes. Perhaps it would help you to think in terms of certain categories.

- Spiritual
- Educational/Intellectual
- Work
- Physical
- Social
- Financial
- Family

When you have completed your list, reread it with these questions in mind:

- Are these purposes for my life consistent with God's will for my life, so far as I understand it?
- Are they consistent with my deepest values?
- Do they help make the world a better place for others?

• Do they help promote the health of our home, the planet Earth, God's creation?

Don't feel that this has to be a once-for-all permanent list. As time goes on and your sense of what God wants you to do with your life is clarified, you can add items, change some, and delete others.

These life purpose statements are important because they set the general direction of our lives. They can help us judge whether our activities are really fulfilling these purposes. When we become confused or discouraged, we can return to these statements to remind ourselves of the purposes we have chosen before God.

However, life purpose statements are not enough because they are not specific. If you actually want to achieve these purposes, you need to proceed to setting goals.

Setting Goals

The apostle Paul exclaimed, "Forgetting what is behind and straining toward what is ahead, *I press on toward the goal* to win the prize for which God has called me . . ." (Phil. 3:13-14, emphasis added). Paul was a man who knew where he was going, and like a track star he ran straight for the finish line. In the process, he spread the gospel of Jesus Christ throughout the Roman empire and transformed Christianity from a Jewish sect into what the Nicene Creed calls the "one holy catholic and apostolic church."

Goals are important. If we know where we're headed, we live our lives with direction and meaning. Our energies are harnessed in the direction God has called us.

Without goals we drift aimlessly. As passive spectators, we can easily be manipulated into conformity with the dying culture of the world. Paul wrote, "Don't let the world around you squeeze you into its own mold, but let God remold your minds from within" (Rom. 12:2 PHILLIPS). As our minds are changed and we develop a clear sense of what God wants us to do and to pursue, the Holy Spirit can transform us into more usable members of God's kingdom.

In the past few years, I have learned about goal setting and have begun to practice it. My experience confirms the words of Maxwell Maltz:

> We are engineered as goal-seeking mechanisms. We are built that way. When we have no personal goal which we are interested in and means something to us, we have to go around in circles, feel lost and find life itself aimless and purposeless. We are built to conquer environment, solve problems, achieve goals and we find no real satisfaction or happiness in life without obstacles to conquer and goals to achieve. People who say that life is not worthwhile are really saying that they themselves have no personal goals which are worthwhile. Get yourself a goal worth working for. Better still, get yourself a project. Decide what you want out of a situation. Always have something to look forward to.[1]

For each of your life purpose statements you should ask: What are some specific goals that will help me move toward the fulfillment of this purpose?

For example, if you listed "Spiritual Growth" as a major life purpose, you might make a list of goals such as these:

- To spend one hour a week in a Bible study class.
- To write in my journal at least fifteen minutes a day.
- To attend church every Sunday.
- To spend fifteen minutes a day in prayer.
- To ask my pastor for a list of spiritual books and to read one a month.

Make a list of goals for each of your major life purposes. You may end up with a very long list—perhaps thirty or forty items. If you attempt that many goals, you are likely to become frustrated and defeated. Therefore, after you have established your goals, mark the ones you consider most important for you to do in the rest of this year, or within the next six months.

When you have reached these goals, then you can add others. As you find yourself reaching your goals, you will gain a sense of achievement. You will feel that you are no longer just drifting or conforming to the expectations of others, but that under the direction of God's Spirit you are in control of your life.

Principles of Goal Setting

It's helpful to remember a few key ideas about goals. Goals should be realistic. In a rush of enthusiasm it is possible to choose too many goals or to choose goals that are beyond our potential. Then, when we fail to reach them, we're tempted to give up and say, "Well, that doesn't work for me," and go back to muddling along through life. It is far better to think in terms of small steps. Choose realistic goals and achieve them. Then, with added confidence, move on.

A friend recently gave me this advice: "If you want to get started jogging, don't set out to run ten miles the first day. If you don't have a heart attack, you will probably be so sore that you will vow never to run again. For the first week, just put on your running shoes every day and take them off again. But do it every day. The next week, put on your running shoes each day and walk once around the block. The next week, walk around the block twice each day. Then the fourth week, start a little jogging." Amusing advice—but realistic.

You could apply the same principle to your spiritual goals. If one of your goals is to establish a regular prayer life, you are better off starting with a goal of five minutes a day than to try for some more heroic goal.

Some people are able to set long-range goals—for five years or ten years or even a lifetime. Then they break these down into yearly, monthly, and daily goals.

When I first began goal setting, I could not plan that far ahead. I was too uncertain of what I really wanted. Winston Churchill once said, "One must always look ahead, but it is difficult to look farther than one can see."

After working with goal setting for a time, I now find it easier to think up to five years ahead.

When you have completed your list of goals and chosen your priorities, check them again against these questions.

- Are these goals consistent with my highest values?
- Are these goals realistic?
- Do they help others?

Whatever time period you choose, once you have established your priority goals, you will need to break them down into more short-range goals. In my system I form goals for a calendar year. Then I break these down into monthly, weekly, and daily goals.

That is the method I used in writing this book. First I outlined the book and discussed the outline with the editor. With the outline approved, I set myself a goal of writing a certain number of pages each day. Other goals included interviewing people who keep journals, attending a journal workshop, reading books and articles on journal writing, rereading my own journals to search for useable material, and reading published journals.

Proceeding in that way, I finished the first draft. Then I set a similar schedule for typing up the second draft. After the editor critiqued that draft, I set new goals for completing the additions and revisions she suggested. The result—a finished book, done step-by-step according to monthly, weekly, and daily goals. By having these small goals as stepping-stones, I could see my progress and keep moving ahead.

Your Journal and Your Goals

I work out my yearly goals in my journal, sometimes ending up with a marked-up, scratched-out page. Then I record these goals at the beginning of a journal volume for ready reference. I leave several pages for monthly and weekly goals.

To keep myself on track, at the beginning of each week I read over my list of yearly and monthly goals and then choose goals for the week. I break these down into daily goals. Life being as uncertain as it is, I often adjust these goals as the week progresses—postponing some, abandoning others, and (rarely) adding some urgent items. Having this written list of short-term goals prevents me from being overwhelmed by work, because it is broken down into small, manageable segments. On the other hand, it keeps me from getting bogged down or wasting time in aimless meandering or following tangents rather than the main tasks at hand.

Without a list like this, I become passive and fall into doing what is *easiest* or most *urgent* rather than what is most *important*.

M. Basil Pennington writes:

> The key to happiness and success in life is a choice of ultimate and immediate goals which are realistic and truly satisfying, a clear grasp of effective means for attaining them and a realistic use of their means.[2]

There is another way I use my journal in connection with my goals. If I am not reaching certain goals, I write about that. How does it feel to be missing those goals? Why did I choose those goals in the first place? Why am I avoiding certain tasks? Am I afraid of failure? Is one goal in conflict with another? Am I not really committed to these goals?

Then I try to work out a plan for either abandoning these goals or finding ways to reach them.

Goal setting can also be a worthwhile activity for families. Sit down together and decide how you would like your family life to be better. Be sure to let the children express their goals. Write down some goals you want to achieve in the next month or in a longer period. From time to time, remind one another of the goals and record your progress in meeting them.

I have been amazed at how some of my visions and goals have come to reality.

Once, during a bus ride across Iowa, I wrote in my journal: "I see myself and my family living happily in a small college town with tree-lined streets." Some years later we began a happy time of life in Northfield, Minnesota, home of *two* small colleges.

During a time of transition I recorded in my journal this conversation with my wife: "You asked me what I really want in life right now. I'd like to be living in a log cabin in the woods, reading and writing." And now that is what I'm doing—while trying to remain open to new visions, new purposes, new goals.

In my pursuit of goals, I can't do everything I want to or even need to do. I must make choices, because there are only twenty-four hours in each day. That brings us to our next subject—time management.

Chapter 10

The Time of Your Life

The apostle Paul directs us to the wise use of our time: "Be careful then how you live, not as unwise people but as wise, making the most of the time, because the days are evil. So do not be foolish, but understand what the will of the Lord is" (Eph. 5:15-17, NRSV).

A key New Testament idea is that of *stewardship*. Today that word brings to mind money and budgets and financial campaigns. But stewardship refers to all of life, including our use of time. So God does not only get a "tithe" of our time, like an hour on Sundays or a few minutes each morning—time that we might think of as "religious." Rather, all of our time is God's. "And whatever you do, whether in word or deed, do it all in the name of the Lord Jesus, giving thanks to God the Father through him" (Col. 3:17).

If you're like most Americans, you are not rich, but you have enough money for the necessities of life; you probably are not homeless or wondering where your next meal is coming from. But, again like most Americans, you suffer from "a poverty of time," the dreadful feeling that there just are not enough hours in the day to do everything you need to do.

Managing our time is difficult, especially when many of us feel we are being pulled in many directions at once. The words of Henri Nouwen in *Sojourners* magazine ring true:

> Just look for a moment at our daily routine. In general we are very
> busy people. We have many meetings to go to, many visits to make,
> many services to lead. Our agendas are filled with appointments,
> our days and weeks filled with engagements, and our years filled

with plans and projects. There is seldom a period in which we do not know what to do, and we move through life in such a constipated way that we do not even take the time to rest and wonder if any of the things we think, say, or do are worth thinking, saying, or doing. We simply go along with the many "musts" and "oughts" which have been handed on to us and live with them as if they were the concrete translations of the gospel of our Lord. Thus we are busy people just like all other busy people, rewarded with the rewards which are rewarded to busy people!"[1]

As Nouwen suggests, the way out of this morass of busyness is to find some solitude to look at your use of time in the light of the goals you have chosen. If you do not control your own time, according to the will of God as you see it, others will control your time for you. Your journal can help you evaluate your present use of time and plan how to make the most of it.

In the preface to his *Journal,* John Wesley wrote:

It was in pursuance of an advice given by Bishop Taylor, in his Rules for Holy Living and Dying, that, about fifteen years ago, I began to take a more exact account than I had done before of the manner wherein I spent my time, writing down how I had employed every hour.[2]

Assessing Your Time

Your first step is to determine how you are using your time now. You might think you already know, but if you actually keep a written record, the results might be surprising. In college, I once was convinced that I was studying sixty hours a week and still was not getting everything done. I did a time analysis and found—to my chagrin—that I had been studying much less than I had thought and was wasting a lot of time.

By keeping track of your time for a week or more, you may find you are spending time on activities that really do not move you toward your goals. It's easy to spend more time with the TV or sports or escape reading or trivial conversation than we realize. (I'm not against any of these activities, but I think the time spent on them should be limited.) If you've thought you just didn't have enough time for some worthwhile activity, you might be able to free up blocks of time you didn't know you had.

To do a time assessment, choose a typical week and keep track of each day's activities, jotting down in a few words the way your time is being used each hour.

You can make a form like the one on page 102 right in your journal. Then you will be able to refer to it later.

When you have done this for seven days, add up the totals to determine your weekly time apportionment. You can use the Weekly Time Summary chart on page 103. I've suggested some common categories of time use. You can add others that apply to your life. After you have compiled your weekly totals, you will have a good idea of how you spend your time.

The next step is to compare your present use of time with your statement of goals worked out in chapter 9. Ask yourself questions like these, and record the answers in your journal.

• Are there any surprises in my use of time?
• Am I spending my time as I think I should be?
• Can I see time being wasted on activities that really do not advance me toward my goals?
• Is there a balance between work, play, and worship?

The last question reminds us that in a balanced life there is time for recreation and relaxation. Without that, we may accomplish less or even become a victim of burnout. By scheduling your relaxation time, along with your other time uses, you will not feel guilty about that time, and you can enjoy it more.

It's also wise to remember that your schedule should be flexible. Jesus said that the sabbath was made for people, not people for the sabbath (see Mark 2:27).

Daily Activity Schedule

Time	Activity
6-7 A.M.	
7-8	
8-9	
9-10	
10-11	
11-12	
12-1 P.M.	
1-2	
2-3	
3-4	
4-5	
5-6	
6-7	
7-8	
8-9	
9-10	
10-11	
11-12	
12-1 A.M.	
1-2	
2-3	
3-4	
4-5	
5-6	

Weekly Time Summary

Activity	Amount of Time
Sleeping	
Working	
Traveling	
Eating	
Shopping	
Recreation	
Reading	
Service to others	
Church activities	
Housework	
Family time	
Prayer and personal devotions	
Spiritual journal	
Unaccounted for	
Other	
Total	168

Your schedule should not enslave you in some rigid framework. It is intended to free you to do what you really want to be doing.

Making the Most of Time

When you've finished analyzing your present use of time, look in your journal again for your list of life purposes and goals. You will be able to achieve your goals only if you build time for them into your schedule. There is no other way.

At writers' conferences I sometimes talk with people who say, "I really want to write, but I never seem to get around to it."

My advice is always the same: "The first step is to set aside some time each day or each week, time in which you sit at your desk and write. Unless you commit a regular block of time to writing, you will never produce much." Some have taken that advice and have put aside a Saturday morning for writing, or a Thursday evening, or two hours every morning—and soon they are on their way to writing success.

The same principle applies to any other activity in your life. If you want to improve your prayer life, you will have to block out time for it in your schedule. If you want to be more physically fit, you will have to find time for walking, jogging, or other activities. If you want to make a difference in your community, you will have to fit that into your schedule. The more you plan your own time, the less you will be manipulated by other people and the more you will be able to progress toward those goals you have chosen.

To deal with the "poverty of time" you may need to do an exercise I call Defenestration, a fancy way of saying "throwing out the window."

Take your journal and, at the top of a page, write "Defenestration." Write about what you need to get rid of in order to make room for what is really important to you. This might include meetings, activities, social events, forms of leisure, relationships, or possessions (it takes time to maintain things). In doing this, you may feel a great sense of relief, or you may experience some pain, because you have to get rid of the good to make room for the best.

The purpose of this exercise is not to make you a slave of a schedule, but to set you free from distractions and time-wasting activities that bless no one.

After you have rethought your time priorities in light of your goals, make another Daily Activity Schedule (like the one on page 102) in your journal. This time use it to plan how you will spend the time of the next day, or the next several days. If you are serious about making the most of your time, you may have to do daily plans for several weeks. After that, certain readjusted time habits will take hold.

If you find yourself reverting to some old time-wasting habits, it might be useful to write about that in your journal. Explore questions like these:

• Why am I not spending time the way I want?
• Why am I settling for second-best in terms of my priorities?
• What changes am I going to make?

When I'm working on a long-term project I find it helpful to record, in list form, what I am doing each day to meet this goal. For example, I might place this heading in my journal: *Five Things I Did Today for My Writing* and record my answers every day. This is one of those simple ideas that keep me focused on my goals, using time effectively.

Some people resist time management, saying, "If I lived like that, I'd be a robot." For me, the opposite is true. I find that if I faithfully follow a schedule, I am not always behind or swamped with work. I actually have more free time for relaxation and spontaneity. And I feel better because my life is moving in the directions I've chosen.

Douglas Rumford states:

A journal helps us clarify our priorities. Life always seems at least a step or two ahead of us. It's easy to lose control. I often turn to my journal as the key to unlock the shackles of the time trap. Reflection enables me to sort out what's important. The commitments that clamor and crowd in on me lose some of their urgency in the light of my basic goals and values. On the other hand, a clear perception of the important matters awakens a new resolve to get on with it.[3]

Chapter 11

Writing for Healing

Twenty-five years after returning from Madagascar, where I had taught English to the children of missionaries and aid workers, I attended the wedding of one of my former students. There I met another student (I'll call her Ann), who exclaimed, "You saved my life!"

"Really?" I responded, amazed. "How did I do that?"

"When you were my eighth-grade English teacher," she began, "you taught us to keep a journal. When we returned to the United States after that year, I was miserable. I had no friends. I didn't know how to act. I was such an outsider. If I hadn't been able to write out my feelings in a journal, I would have committed suicide."

And now Ann is happily married, with two lovely children.

Many people, like Ann, begin journaling in crisis. The journal becomes a place to release emotions, make sense of the situation, and find healing. New scientific studies have established that people who have experienced some kind of difficult experience—illness, grief, divorce, job loss, relationship problems—come through it better, with greater health and well-being, if they write about it in a journal or tell their story to another person.

The premier researcher about writing as a way of healing is James W. Pennebaker, professor of psychology at Southern Methodist University. In a series of experiments he found that people who wrote fifteen minutes a day about difficult life events gained greater mental and physical health. His conclusions have been verified by other researchers working with people with both physical and mental problems.

In his book *Opening Up: The Healing Power of Expressing Emotions*, Pennebaker says:

Translating our thoughts into language is psychologically and physically beneficial. When people write about major upheavals, they begin to organize and understand them. Writing about the thoughts and feelings of traumas, then, forces individuals to bring together the many facets of overwhelmingly complicated events. Once people can distill complex experiences into more understandable passages, they can begin to move beyond the trauma.[1]

In an article in *American Health*, "Writing Your Wrongs," Dr. Pennebaker describes the kind of writing that promotes health:

Whatever your topic, it's critical to explore both the objective experience and your feelings about it. Let go and express your deepest emotions, what you feel about it and why you feel that way. Write continuously; don't worry about grammar, spelling, or sentence structure. If you run out of things to say or reach a mental block, just repeat what you have already written.[2]

Dr. Pennebaker adds a warning:

I should point out that exploring your deepest thoughts and feelings on paper is not a panacea. If you're coping with death, divorce, or some other major trauma, you won't feel better instantly after writing. You should, however have a clearer understanding of your feelings and emotions as well as your objective situation. In other words, writing should give you some distance and perspective on your life. And that can lead to positive changes in your physical and mental health.[3]

The *Journal of the American Medical Association* reported a study in which patients with asthma and rheumatoid arthritis showed a marked reduction of their symptoms after writing in their journals about stressful events.[4]

Research evidence also indicates that writing in a journal is as effective as talking to a therapist.[5] And the journal has some advantages. It is always available. It is inexpensive. It may allow greater openness. Dr. Pennebaker says, "One reason why writing is so potent is that usually when we start to tell somebody about some personal thing, we're watching their face very closely to see how they react. If we see any sign that the other person is shocked or disapproving, we immediately start to change the story."[6]

In *Writing as a Way of Healing,* Louise DeSalvo writes:

> Writing about traumatic or troubling life experiences initially unleashes difficult, conflicting emotions. In the long run, though, we feel better emotionally and are healthier and achieve a level of understanding of our lives that only writing can provide. Safe writing—writing what we already know or understand, writing that is superficial—won't help us grow, either as people or as writers. For our writing to be healing, we must encounter something that puzzles, confuses, troubles, or pains us.[7]

The research of Dr. Pennebaker as well as the stories of many individuals point to the fact that writing in a journal can be one channel for God's healing to reach us—along with medication, counseling, and other therapies.

The Healing Journal

Any writing you do in a journal can help you move toward greater maturity and well-being, but in this chapter I'd like to suggest ways the journal can be used for healing in some specific situations. Here I'm using *healing* in a comprehensive way to include anything that contributes to overcoming wounds and blockages that prevent you from becoming all you could be.

Identifying Your Wounds

In your journal, write a list of seven-year life periods, as many as you need.

0-7
8-14
15-21
22-28
29-35
36-42
43-49
50-56
57-63
64-70
71-77
78-85

Taking one period at a time, reenter that age and list any wounds or hurts you received—mental, physical, or spiritual. These could be illnesses, disappointments, accidents, losses, hurtful relationships, or a spiritual crisis.

When you finish all of your seven-year periods, look over the list to see any patterns. When did much of the hurt occur? What kinds of wounds predominate? Write out your thoughts and feelings.

Healing of Memories

When you're ready, choose one or more of these experiences to explore in greater depth, following Dr. Pennebaker's advice of writing fifteen minutes a day about this topic for at least four days. Write what happened, how you felt then, how you feel now. Ask God to bring forgiveness and healing as needed.

As time goes on, choose other of these wounds to write about. If some are too difficult and you do not feel ready to write about these, let them be for now. Trust your own inner wisdom.

Although an exercise like this may bring to the surface unremembered pain, this awareness is the beginning of healing. If you should find yourself dealing with more pain than you can handle by yourself, seek out a friend, pastor, or counselor to talk things over with. The combination of writing and talking is a powerful means of healing.

For a Christian perspective on inner healing see *Healing of Memories* by Dennis Linn and Matthew Linn and *Healing the Eight Stages of Life* by Matthew Linn, Sheila Fabricant, and Dennis Linn.

Dealing with Depression

Millions of us—probably all of us at times—suffer from depression, whether we call it the blues, the blahs, or just being down. When we're depressed, we feel sad, lackluster, weary, hopeless—even despairing. When depression is serious and long-lasting, it usually signals the need for medical treatment and counseling. But for the ordinary, everyday level of depression, the journal is a big help, and even with serious clinical depression, writing can supplement medication and talk therapy.

I've never suffered from a clinical level of depression, but I have struggled with the more ordinary garden-variety depression, and I've found a number of ways that writing helps me cope. One or more of these techniques almost always produces a lighter, more optimistic mood and brighter feelings.

- Write out how you're feeling, as exactly as you can. How does the depression feel? Where do you feel it? Identify the thoughts that are depressing you. See if you can analyze the origins of your depression (you may not be able to immediately).
- Write out your depression in a letter to God, as the psalmists do. Let God have it! God is strong enough to take it.
- Turn away from your depression and write this heading in your journal: "Tell Me All the Good News You Can Think of." Then list everything that you can genuinely consider good news.
- Keep a Gratitude Journal (see chapter 4).
- I begin each morning by writing this affirmation: "This will be a good day." Then I list everything I can look forward to, based on the old idea that "every day is a good day." This exercise helps establish a good frame of mind for the day and keeps me from being dominated by my To Do list.
- Each day write about your "peak experiences"—the moments

when you feel alive, positive, happy. There is some evidence that writing about peak experiences generates more of them.

• If you're going through a particularly stressful period of your life, look back over some earlier chapters when things were going better and write about those. Write about what was life-enhancing, write about what you loved. This can help restore your perspective.

• Copy into your journal Bible verses, prayers, other inspiring quotations that help lift your spirits.

My experience is that exercises like these, repeated over time, are indeed healing.

Grief and Loss

Dr. James W. Pennebaker investigated people who were coping with the death of a spouse. He found that those who talked or wrote about the experience remained more healthy. He also found, "The more people prayed about their deceased spouse, the healthier they were. Prayer, in fact, worked the same way as talking to friends about the death. It is easy to see why this is true: Prayer is a form of disclosure or confiding."[8]

When you are mourning the loss of a loved one, it's important to give words to your sorrow. One advantage of writing in a journal is that it is always there, and it may keep you from wearing out your friends or family members.

In chapter 6, I described how I had found healing by writing a letter to a friend who died in a foreign country.

After the deaths of both my parents I have written a series of letters to them, saying things I had not been able to say to them earlier.

A more difficult, but potentially beneficial, technique is to write a letter from the deceased person to you, having them say what you wish they would say to you.

You might also want to write about a treasured relationship, naming the steps, recalling especially happy times.

Again, copy into your journal the prayers and other quotations that you find especially comforting and strengthening.

In *Writing as a Way of Healing,* Louise DeSalvo stresses the value of writing our grief stories:

> Because our writing, our work of art, is a concrete object, it becomes a memorial and a testimony to the resolution of the mourning process. And to the lost person and the lost self. By writing, we celebrate, too, our courage and survival. Engaging in writing, in creative work, then, permits us to pass from numbness to feeling, from denial to acceptance, from conflict and chaos to order and resolution, from rage and loss to profound growth, from grief to joy.[9]

We can use the same techniques that work for grieving the loss of a loved one to deal with any kind of loss.

Job Loss

Colleagues of Dr. Pennebaker found that people who were going through job loss or transition fared better if they wrote about the experience.[10] This was also my experience. I was working for a publisher that went through some dramatic changes that adversely affected my job. I could see that it was a race between whether I would quit or get fired. I began to look for other job opportunities, but when every door seemed to be closed I went into the deepest depression of my life.

During this time I talked things over with my wife, with several good friends in person and by phone, and met with a career counselor. I also made good use of my journal, where I wrote about the work I did in each chapter of my life, how it went, how I felt about it. I made lists of potential jobs, both inside my field and outside it. I wrote out my feelings of fear, of failure, of worry. I listened for God's call.

Both the talking and the writing helped move me past my stuck place and beyond my feelings of despair. And after a few months I was ready to write my letter of resignation and move on.

Lifestyle Changes

Changes in lifestyle or habits are notoriously difficult to make, even when we know we ought to do them. At this time of writing, I'm trying to take off twenty undesired pounds. (Losing weight is easy for me; in the past thirty years I've lost hundreds of pounds!) Actually for me losing weight is not easy, just simple: I know I have to eat less and exercise more. My problem is maintaining that simple method for more than two hours.

In the midst of the battle I turn to my trusty journal. I've written my reasons for wanting to lose weight—all good ones—so I can review them when I forget. I've written about what has worked for me in previous attempts to lose weight (and what has not). I keep a food log. I write ideas for coping with temptations. I maintain an exercise log.

Does the journal writing help? I think so. The jury is still out and most of the twenty pounds are still there under my belt, but I'm hopeful.

On a more serious note, for dealing with alcohol or drug addictions, I recommend the book *Journeynotes: Writing for Recovery and Spiritual Growth* (out-of-print) by Richard Solly and Roseann Lloyd. It contains many suggestions for journal-writing exercises that are associated with the Twelve Steps of Alcoholics Anonymous but can be used by anyone in recovery.

These are only a sampling of the many ways you can use writing in a journal as a way of healing.

For further ideas on writing for healing, I recommend the books and tapes by Kathleen Adams, founder of The Center for Journal Therapy, especially *The Write Way to Wellness: A Workbook for Healing and Change* and the accompanying tape. You might also check out her Web site: www.journaltherapy.com. Louise DeSalvo's *Writing as a Way of Healing* (Beacon Press, 2000) contains much compassionate wisdom on how we can shape healing stories and care for ourselves in the process.

I believe that once you begin, you will find your own ways to use writing as a way of being in touch with God's healing presence and power.

Chapter 12

Problems along the Way

Let's say you've made a beginning in journal keeping. You have bought a journal, and you've made a commitment to write in it. You've begun keeping a Daily Record. You use your journal as an aid to caring for your soul. From time to time you use your journal for looking backward or looking forward and for healing.

You're on the journal road to spiritual growth. But what are some problems you might meet along the way?

The Issue of Privacy

To be of maximum benefit to you, your journal should be the place where you can write anything—including the thoughts and feelings you do not wish to share with other people. That's one of the great advantages of a journal. When you write in it, you can take off your social mask and be yourself.

But what if someone should read these honest expressions or explorations? You might be misunderstood or what you have written could be used against you in some way. There is also the chance that someone might be deeply hurt by what you write. Therefore, you should think through the issue of privacy and be prepared to cope with it in some way.

If you live alone, the issue is fairly simple. The odds of someone picking up your journal are slight. It may be enough for you to put a sign on your journal, as one person did.

Now I lay me down to sleep.
I pray the Lord my soul to keep.
If I should die before I wake,
Please throw my journal in the lake!

If you live with others—family or friends—you may need to take more exacting measures to preserve the privacy of your journal.

If you can trust those you live with, you could discuss openly the fact that you are keeping a journal and that you desire to keep it private. My wife and I both keep journals, and we simply would not snoop in one another's journals. That is part of our faithfulness to one another.

If you think that informing others about your journal would only arouse their curiosity, as an added precaution you could keep your journal in a locked drawer. It certainly is unwise to let your journal lie around to tempt others.

One man felt he could not leave his journal in his desk at work or at home without its being read, so he kept it in the trunk of his car. I hope you don't have to take such extreme measures!

It may be wise to use some sort of code for certain entries—the names of individuals, for example. Just be sure you will be able to decode it years later.

In addition to his widely published journal, John Wesley kept a secret journal in an elaborate code that used shorthand, letters, symbols, and dots and dashes. It has only recently been decoded!

If you keep your journal on a computer, you can protect it with a password.

Finding Enough Time to Write

When talking with other people about journal keeping, the most frequent problem I hear is, "I just don't seem to have enough time." This issue was discussed in detail in chapter 3, but I will add a few reminders here.

Establishing a set time to write every day is probably the best way to ensure that you will write regularly.

Think in terms of short periods of time, if necessary. Don't wait until you have an hour or two for writing. Even five or ten minutes is worthwhile.

Don't feel you must write every day. Many people write once or twice a week and still find the journal valuable. If you really can't write every day, then write when you can.

Maintaining Interest

Perhaps you've been keeping a journal for months or even years, but you now find it has gone stale for you. What can you do?

In chapter 3, you were encouraged to write a statement about why you are keeping a journal. Reread this statement from time to time to remind yourself of your original goal.

Write about why you are not writing in your journal. Maybe you will find some clues about your own priorities and how you are spending your time. You may decide to do some reordering in your life.

Try making some changes in the way you keep your journal. Write at a different time of day or in a different place. Use a different pen or different book. Try word processing your journal or taping it. A change like this, even if only temporary, may be enough to give you a fresh burst of energy.

You can also experiment with changing the content of your writing. If you've been writing mainly your Daily Record, try some of the exercises in chapters 6-11. If your journal has been mostly introspective—analyzing yourself and your ideas—try focusing outward for a while and write about other people. Describe places and events. If you've been writing mainly about the present, try exploring the past or even the future.

It may be helpful to get together with other people who keep journals, or even with one other person. You can discuss the problems of journaling and what you do that works. If you feel comfortable doing so, share parts of your journal with one another.

In many areas of the country there are classes or workshops in journaling. Such an event may renew your interest and offer new ideas for journal writing.

There are many good books on journal writing from various perspectives. Most of them have many journal "prompts" or exercises to get you writing in new ways. You can choose those that seem most intriguing or appropriate for you. Some books I have found helpful: *Journal to the Self: Twenty-Two Paths to Personal Growth* by Kathleen Adams; and *Keeping a Journal You Love* and *A Year in the Life: Journaling for Self-Discovery,* both by Sheila Bender.

If you have access to the Internet, search for the word *journal* plus words like *therapy* or *writing.* You'll be led to sites that contain journal exercises, recommended resources for journaling, and chat rooms in which you can "talk" with other journal writers.

One way to enrich your journal keeping—and your spiritual growth—is to read some of the great published journals. Reading them will give you insights into the spiritual life and into some people worth knowing.

People reveal themselves in a unique way in their journals. Louis Untermeyer states:

> When we read a diary, we are not merely looking over a man's shoulder. We are looking into his inmost mind, his hidden heart; here everything is forthright and without subterfuge. There is no critic to frown, no censor to intimidate; no editor can come between the writer and his uninhibited thoughts. Emotions find their expression without fumbling for the precise word, although the perfect phrase is achieved. Whatever happens is usually described just after it has occurred—everything is spontaneous, unpremeditated, and completely convincing.[1]

A large library will contain hundreds of published journals, usually under the headings *journal, diary,* or *notebooks.* A trip to your local bookstore will turn up several. For Further Reading in this book suggests some of the journals that are most worthwhile for what they reveal about spiritual growth. You will also be directed to some guidebooks, should you wish to go further into the fascinating world of the journal.

As you read these journals (it is the kind of reading that is easy to do in snatches) you will probably get some ideas for your own journal keeping. You may want to copy passages that interest you so you can retain them in your own journal. Some of the older journals offer an easy and fascinating door into history.

If none of the above ideas work, you may just choose to take a vacation from your journal. There is a rhythm in life of engagement and withdrawal, work and rest. One can apply that to a journal, too. You could say, "I give myself permission *not* to write in my journal for one month." Then stop writing—and don't feel guilty about it!

Spending Too Much Time Writing

While most people have trouble finding enough time for journal writing, a few individuals find themselves so caught up in a journal that it takes hours of their time every day. If you should find yourself spending too much time in your journal, or spending time that should be invested in other activities, ask yourself a few questions: "Why is the journal so important to me?" "Are there better ways I should be spending some of this time?"

Perhaps the best thing to do is to set yourself a time limit: "I will write for only half an hour, and during that time I will try to concentrate on what is most important for me."

Having Nothing to Say

What if you sit down to write and your mind is a blank? You have nothing to say.

You could start by writing about boredom! How does it feel? Write about why your life is so dull that you have nothing to say. Better yet, write about what you can do about this.

Ask yourself, "What can I do to enrich my life so that I have something to say?" The answer is not to search out an exotic or immoral experience. Go to the library. Read some good books. Browse in magazines. See a new movie. Visit someone in a hospital or nursing home. Take a walk in the woods. Sit in the park and watch children play. Take a course at a community college. Get involved in a service group at your church or in your community. Make some new friends. *Do something,* and you'll have something to write about.

Becoming Overly Introspective

I believe a journal is a gift of God. Like any gift, it can be misused. It is possible for me to become overly absorbed in myself, going around and around analyzing myself and probing my motives or dwelling on unpleasant experiences.

If you feel this happening to you, you could choose to spend less time writing in your journal. Or you could change the focus of your writing. One friend recently stopped writing in her journal because there was a troublesome situation in her life, and she was spending hours dwelling on this problem and ending up upset and depressed. I suggested that she continue to write in her journal, but that she write about everything else in her life *except* that problem, especially focusing on the joys in her life.

Douglas Rumford underlines the importance of remaining basically positive in journal writing:

> Discipline yourself to write positively. The aim of the journal is to generate the energy to be an overcomer. State the facts, record your negative feelings honestly, but then seek out the promise.[2]

The Bible does encourage us to examine ourselves, but this does not mean we should become preoccupied with ourselves. Lowell Erdahl explains the distinction:

> Periodic self-examination is a necessity; perpetual self-preoccupation is a curse. Self-examination is an occasional glimpse in the

mirror. Self-preoccupation is endlessly looking to see if we are beautiful enough.[3]

You can deliberately choose to turn your attention away from your "inner workings" by writing about other people, the world of nature, or events in the outer world. If this period of your life is particularly stressful or unhappy, you may find balance and perspective by writing about earlier chapters of your life or using some of the exercises in chapter 9.

Should it happen that you feel you are in any sense losing control over your journal writing, discuss this with your pastor or another counselor.

Although a few people are inclined to be overly introspective, most of us have the opposite problem. In our overly busy society, when we are pulled in many directions and there are many demands on our time, our problem is not that we think too much. Our problem is that we are too busy to think at all. This is one reason why a journal can be such a helpful practice.

Chapter 13

Harvesting Your Journal

The act of writing is beneficial because it causes you to reflect and focuses your mind. But if you preserve your writing in a journal, it can have still greater benefits. Your journal will have additional value when you read it and work with the contents.

Reading Your Journal

The most basic step in "harvesting" your journal is simply to read what you have written. When should you do this? Anytime you feel like it! However, certain times seem especially appropriate.

- At the end of a week or month
- At the end of a year
- On your birthday, to review the past year
- When you complete a particular "volume" of your journal

There is one exception to this. If your journal records a particularly painful time, you probably will want to wait until you feel ready to relive those memories. A friend who wrote extensively in his journal while experiencing serious mental-health issues still does not feel ready to read these sections of his journal.

One common reaction to reading one's journal is to think, "These thoughts are trivial and stupid. How could I have written such drivel!" I kept a journal for a few months when I was fifteen. Then at age eighteen I read the journal and decided it was so juvenile that I destroyed it. Now I wish I had the record of my thoughts and feelings at that age.

In the process of writing this book I read some of my earliest journals. I was surprised to see that I am wrestling today with some of the same questions and problems that I struggled with thirty years ago! In one sense this is frustrating, yet I realize these are *my* questions and *my* problems.

Thomas Merton wrote in his journal:

> Keeping a journal has taught me that there is not so much new in your life as you sometimes think. When you reread your journal, you find out that your latest discovery is something you already found out about five years ago. Still it is true that one penetrates deeper and deeper into the same ideas and the same experiences.[1]

In addition to noting some continuity in your life, you may also be surprised to see how much you have changed in certain ways. You might notice that your present memories are not very accurate because they have been colored by what has happened between the original event and the present time. I observed this when I reread my first impressions of Madagascar.

Rereading some of the more stressful experiences of one's life can be uncomfortable, but I usually find that reading my journals is an energizing experience. I don't know all the reasons for this, but I suspect that as we become more integrated within ourselves, more whole, less energy is spent on destructive or defensive emotions. This releases energy that can be used for living and working in the present.

One feeling people often have when they read their journals is gratitude. A friend says:

> When I reread my journals, I am often fascinated by my own reaction to things. Sometimes I think "How could I ever have felt that way?" or even "I'm glad I had that much sense." Or I can relive a period of depression or frustration and feel absolutely glorious that "Out of it all the Lord delivered me."

You may simply want to read your journal and see what strikes you. But if you want to evaluate it more intensely, you could ask yourself questions like these:

- What do I write about most often—the past, the present, ideas, events, other people?
- Are there significant areas of my life that are not finding their way into my journal? Is there any special meaning in this?
- How frequently am I writing? Am I satisfied with this? If not, what am I going to do about it?
- What features of my journal writing do I want to continue?
- Are there ways I could make better use of my journal?

Sometimes I reread a portion of my journals with a specific question in mind, usually growing out of some personal dissatisfaction. If I'm feeling I haven't accomplished anything recently, I will go back and make a list of what I actually have accomplished. Usually I find that the feeling was not reliable; the journal tells the truth about what I accomplished. Or if I'm feeling that my life is dull and all I'm doing is working, I go back to my journals and ask: What has been life-enhancing? What were the enjoyable times? If I'm feeling that I'm not learning anything, I'll look back to see what books I read. What other learning experiences did I have? Almost always I find that reading my journal corrects my feelings and brings me a more balanced perspective. Of course, it also sometimes goes the other way. When I was in graduate school, I was feeling sorry for myself, saying, "Poor me! I'm knocking myself out studying sixty hours a week!" I read back in my journals and did some calculating and found I was not working as hard as I thought.

Journal reading can be a reality check. Memory and feelings are not always accurate. The journal, with a record captured close to the moment, can reveal the truth—assuming you were honest in your writing.

End-of-the-Year Summary

A natural time for examining your life is at the end of one year and the beginning of another. This can be done for (1) the calendar year or (2) on your birthday for your personal year.

For many years I have spent some time between Christmas and New Year's Day reviewing the past year and making plans for the next one.

As I look back I answer these questions, usually in lists rather than in detail:

- What were the major events of this year, month by month? (I answer this from memory and by looking back at my journal for the year.)
- What did I accomplish? (For me this is mainly a list of writings completed or published, but it also includes speaking or teaching or family activities.)
- What traveling did I do?
- Who are the people I feel closest to at this point in my life?
- Did I make any new friends this past year?
- What was the most important reading I did?
- What were my greatest joys?
- In what ways did I grow?
- In what ways was I able to use my gifts to serve others?
- What did I learn from this year?

I usually work on these questions for perhaps a half-hour at a time for several days. When I feel I have a sense of the year past, I turn my thoughts to the coming year. I ask questions like these:

- What do I look forward to in the coming year?
- What do I hope for in the coming year?
- What changes do I want to make?
- What are my goals for the coming year?
- How will I use my gifts to serve others in the coming year?
- Is God saying anything to me about the year to come?

By reviewing my answers to these questions frequently during the year, I keep myself headed in the direction I have chosen.

Bringing Things Forward

A journal-keeping practice that you may find helpful is "bringing things forward." When you find some especially interesting insight while rereading a journal, copy it in your present journal and add some thoughts, showing how your thinking has been reinforced or changed.

For example, you might write: "In June, 1998, I wrote in my journal _____. Today I feel _____.

Indexing

When I finish a volume of my journal, I read it and index it by marking the more significant passages in the margin. (In the light of rereading, some of the "dailyness" of the journal entries does not seem as significant as when I wrote it.) Indexing helps me locate the more valuable entries.

As I read, I put one of these letters in the margin:

I   for an *insight* into myself, others, or life
Q   for a *quotation* I may want to use later
S   for a *struggle,* something I'm wrestling with
W   for a *writing* idea
A   for an *anecdote* or incident I may want to use in my writing
C   for a *clue,* something that is worth further thought
TD for things *to do,* some actions I should take

You could use these initials or devise some of your own—F for *family,* W for *work,* or whatever will help you locate the most significant or meaningful passages in your journal.

Gleaning

The following method of "gleaning" from a journal is one I learned from a Canadian writer, Maxine Hancock. She calls it "culling." It is especially valuable for writers, speakers, or teachers, but others might also experiment with it.

After your journal has been indexed, go through and type or write on three-by-five-inch cards any quotations, anecdotes, or ideas you may want to use in the future. Put a heading at the top of the card, such as "Prayer," "Spiritual Discipline," "Christmas," or "Short Story Idea." Then file these alphabetically. These ideas can also be used with a database program on a personal computer.

This gleaning from the journal takes some time, but it does make the contents of the journal readily accessible for further use.

Assembling Entries

At some point you may want to go through a journal or several journals and type up a series of entries on a particular topic. This helps you see the flow of your experience and thought and can be a springboard to further writing. If you have kept your journal on a computer, it's easy to copy and paste your entries into a new file.

When I felt the need to come to terms with a certain job I had, I skimmed back through five years of my journals and identified the passages dealing with that work. I first created the index, listing the dates of the entries and their topic. Then I went back and typed up those entries, shaping them into a coherent story: how I got the job, how it was at the beginning, what I accomplished, the highs and lows, the changes that occurred in the company, and why I decided to leave. By creating a coherent story, I made peace with it and found some inner healing.

Sharing Your Journal

Elizabeth O'Connor says, "Always write the journal for yourself. Though it is true that you may want to share it, never write it with this in mind."[2] The reason, of course, is that if you are writing for an audience you will do too much conscious or unconscious censoring. This defeats one of the main benefits of journaling—the ability to express yourself freely and honestly.

This book has stressed that your journal should be a *private* book. However, there are times when you may want to share at least parts of your journal with others.

One way to do this is through letters or e-mails. Letter writing becomes easier when you make use of your journal, and your letters will be richer for it. A glance back at the past weeks or months of your journal will give you plenty of good material to share in a letter.

As mentioned in a previous chapter, you may find a journal group helpful. In such a group, people can read aloud those entries they feel ready to share. An important rule, however, is that no one should be pressured into sharing. Respect one another's privacy.

You may also want to read portions of your journal to family or friends. However, never use your journal as a weapon to manipulate others or to try to change them. Share only what might be helpful or interesting to the other person.

Another way to share your journal is to type up portions of it, editing as you go. When I have a sufficient block of time, I want to do this with my journal of our years in Madagascar, especially those sections that deal with the land and the people and the experiences our family had there. Because our children were quite young then, a record like this will help to nourish their memories of this experience.

Some parents create a birthday gift for a child by writing a record of the most important events in that child's previous year.

On my daughter's twenty-first birthday, as part of the celebration, I read aloud my entries from each of her previous birthdays.

One year I went through my journals and wrote down the most important events of each month. Then I shared it with the family on New Year's Day. This was a good way to relive the experiences of the year and build family memories.

Writing for Publication

For many people—including myself—the journal has been a practice field for writing. It's a safe place for learning how to put experiences and thoughts into words. I have gone back into my journals to find material that I could develop into poems, articles, stories, and parts of books, but it's better at first to write just for yourself, with no thought of publication.

When you feel the desire to move toward sharing some of your thoughts and experiences through publication, you have to think in a different way from just writing what comes to mind. You need to think more about the audience, the reader and his or her interests and needs. You have to think more about the craft of writing, about choosing words, shaping sentences, forming paragraphs that will attract and hold the reader. In short, you need to learn to *rewrite*.

If you decide to move from journal writing to writing for publication, there is much to learn. But many ways of learning to write are available to you: classes at community colleges or universities, correspondence courses, Internet classes, and still one of the best—books—available at your library or bookstores or online. A few of my favorites are listed under "Creative Writing" in For Further Reading at the back of this book.

Bon Voyage

We have come a long way on the journal road. I hope this book has convinced you of the benefits of journal keeping and has stimulated you to begin using a journal for spiritual growth.

Enjoy your journal. Let your journal writing be sabbath time in the presence of God. Heed the words of 2 Peter 3:18: "Grow in the grace and knowledge of our Lord and Savior Jesus Christ. To him be glory both now and forever! Amen."

Guide for Forming
a Journal Group

Journal writing is one of the ultimate solitary activities, yet in order to develop the habit and maintain the writing, some people find a small support group helpful. Such a group can work through *How to Keep a Spiritual Journal* and help one another get started in journal writing.

The group may be as small as two and probably should not be much larger than a dozen. You can choose to write in class or to write at home and use the class time only for discussion of the book and the journal-writing process.

A few basic ground rules for a journaling group:

1. Everyone who comes should commit to writing in a journal at least a few days a week.

2. Absolute confidentiality is required. No one should be pressured into reading their journals aloud. If people know they're going to have to read their entries to the group, they will begin to censor and one of the benefits of journaling—total honesty—will be lost. I suggest that the only exception might be a kind of "show and tell" time in the last session in which participants could choose a paragraph or two to share with the group.

3. What is useful is to discuss the process of journal writing. After participants have had an opportunity, at home or in the group, to try a particular journal exercise, discuss, "How did that go for you? What worked? What problems did you have?" Discuss any difficulties you have with maintaining the discipline of journal writing.

4. I encourage you to experiment with doing some writing in the group meeting. My experience is that many people find that writing

is easier that way, that there is some group energy that makes the writing flow more readily.

I will suggest a basic outline for six weekly meetings. I choose six weeks because some people think it takes about that long to develop a new habit, to make journal writing a part of your daily life. Of course, your group can adjust this to meet their own needs.

One alternative would be to use a weekend retreat, with session 1 on Friday evening, sessions 2-4 on Saturday with free time for private work, and sessions 5-6 on Sunday.

Preliminary Meeting
- Distribute the copies of *How to Keep a Spiritual Journal.*
- Share your interest and experience with journal writing. What brings you here?
- Discuss the ground rules given above.
- Ask participants to read chapters 1-4 in *How to Keep a Spiritual Journal.*

Session 1
- Discuss chapters 1-4. What benefits do participants hope to get from journal writing? What plans do they have for beginning? Which elements of the Daily Record do they think they will include in their journals? Ask for any questions group members have at this point.
- Consider writing "Your Personal Contract" on p. 36 (Assure people they can always modify this commitment).
- In-class writing: Do the exercise in flow-writing on p. 35. Ask participants how that went for them.
- Reading: Assign chapters 5, 6, and 12.
- At-home writing: Ask participants to keep a Daily Record at least three or four times in the coming week.

Session 2
- Ask people to share how they did with keeping the Daily Record in the past week.

• Discuss chapters 5, 6, and 12. Be sure to spend some time on the issue of privacy and how participants are handling that.

• In-class writing: Choose one or more of the exercises in chapter 6—perhaps "Unmailed Letters." Take a few minutes afterward to discuss how the exercise worked for people.

• Reading: Assign chapter 7.

• At-home writing: Suggest that participants continue the Daily Record while experimenting with one or more of the techniques in chapter 6.

Session 3

• Check in with one another by sharing your journal-writing experience of the past week. If some people are having problems, pool your wisdom to seek answers.

• Discuss chapter 7. How will group members use the journal to care for their souls?

• In-class writing: Do one or more of the exercises in spiritual reading and prayer. If you do the spiritual reading exercise, have Bibles on hand.

• Reading: Assign chapter 8.

• At-home writing: Suggest that participants continue the Daily Record, but concentrate on adding one or more of the soul-care exercises.

Session 4

• Share people's experiences with journaling in the past week, especially the exercises in spiritual reading and prayer.

• Discuss chapter 8.

• In-class writing: Choose one or more exercises from chapter 8. "The Chapters of Your Life" is a good place to begin.

• Reading: Assign chapters 9 and 10.

• At-home writing: Suggest that participants choose one or more of the exercises from chapter 8 to add to their journal writing for the week.

Session 5

• Allow time at the beginning of the session for people to check in and share their experiences with journal writing during the past week.

• Discuss chapter 9.

• In-class writing: Choose which of the exercises you will do in class. I suggest those under "Envisioning Your Future."

• Reading: Assign chapter 11.

• At-home writing: Remind participants to continue their Daily Record, while adding in one or more of the exercises on "Looking Forward."

• Discuss whether you want to have a "read-aloud" time at the end of the next session in which people read excepts from their journals. If some members wish to do this, ask them to prepare a paragraph or two.

Session 6

• Share your journal writing of the past week. If people are having any problems, ask other group members to offer suggestions from their own experience.

• Discuss chapter 11. Ask participants to identify how they're planning to use these exercises, if they feel comfortable sharing this information.

• In-class writing: Choose one or more exercises to do in class. "Identifying Your Wounds" would be a good place to begin.

• Allow time for those who wish to read from their journals to do so.

• Discuss how the past six weeks have gone for the group. Decide whether some members wish to continue meeting.

For Further Reading

The following are books related to spiritual growth and journal keeping that I especially recommend. Not all of these are currently in print but may be found in libraries, used bookstores, or at on-line bookstores.

Spiritual Growth

Brussat, Frederic and Mary Ann. *Spiritual Literacy: Reading the Sacred in Everyday Life* (New York: Simon and Schuster Touchstone, 1998) and *Spiritual Rx: Prescriptions for Living a Meaningful Life* (New York: Hyperion, 2000). Both these books are treasure-houses of inspiration and practices for spiritual growth, including journal exercises.

Foster, Richard. *Celebration of Discipline* (San Francisco: HarperCollins, 1978). An excellent guide to spiritual disciplines by a contemporary Quaker writer.

Linn, Dennis and Matthew Linn. *Healing of Memories* (New York: Paulist Press, 1974). Two Roman Catholic priests discuss prayer and confession as steps to inner healing.

Linn, Dennis and Sheila Fabricant and Matthew Linn. *Healing the Eight Stages of Life* (New York: Paulist Press, 1988). Prayerful ways to inner healing based on the human development theories of Erik Erikson.

Nouwen, Henri J. M. *Reaching Out* (Garden City, N.Y: Doubleday, 1975). A contemporary writer describes the three movements of the spiritual life: from loneliness to solitude, from hostility to hospitality, and from illusion to prayer.

O'Connor, Elizabeth. *Search for Silence* (San Diego: Lura Media, 1986). An important guide to prayer and contemplation that includes journal exercises.

_____.*Letters to Scattered Pilgrims* (San Francisco: HarperCollins, 1979). Contemporary letters of spiritual counsel, including several that speak of journal writing.

Journals

There are hundreds of published journals that make for fascinating reading. Here is a sampling:

Asbury, Francis. *Selections from the Journal of Francis Asbury,* ed. J. Manning Potts (Nashville: The Upper Room, 1952). An early Methodist circuit rider and church organizer records his experiences in revolutionary America.

Borland, Hal. *Hal Borland's Book of Days* (New York: Alfred A. Knopf, 1976). An American naturalist shares daily observations on the world of nature.

Brainerd, David. *The Life and Diary of David Brainerd,* ed. Jonathan Edwards; newly ed. Phillip E. Howard, Jr. (Chicago: Moody Press, 1945). The journal of a great missionary to Native Americans during the colonial period.

Derleth, August. *Countryman's Journal* (New York: Duell, Sloan, and Pearce, 1963) and *Village Daybook: A Sac Prairie Journal* (Chicago: Pellegrini & Cudahy, 1947). In these books one of my favorite journal writers describes the natural history and small-town life of central Wisconsin.

Elliot, Jim. *The Journals of Jim Elliot,* ed. Elisabeth Elliot (Old Tappan, N.J.: Revell, 1978). Glimpses into the heart of a contemporary missionary martyred by the Auca tribe of South America.

Fenn, Charles. *Journal of a Voyage to Nowhere* (New York: W. W. Norton & Co., 1971). A modern-day Robinson Crusoe who was marooned on an atoll in the Indian Ocean kept a record of his struggle to stay alive.

Frank, Anne. *Anne Frank: The Diary of a Young Girl* (Garden City, N.Y.: Doubleday, 1967). A 20th century classic by a young Jewish girl who lived and died in Nazi-occupied Holland.

Hammarskjöld, Dag. *Markings,* trans. Leif Sjöberg and W. H. Auden (New York: Alfred A. Knopf, 1965). When the secretary-general of the United Nations was killed in a plane crash, he left behind this record of his spiritual journey.

Hillesum, Etty. *An Interrupted Life* (New York: Pantheon Books, 1981). Spiritual testimony of a twenty-nine-year-old Jewish woman who died in the Holocaust.

Hoffer, Eric. *Working and Thinking on the Waterfront* (New York: Harper & Row, 1969). A San Francisco longshoreman-philosopher shares his observations and insights in a journal kept in 1958-59.

Koren, Elisabeth. *The Diary of Elisabeth Koren,* trans. David T. Nelson (Northfield, Minn.: Norwegian-American Historical Assoc., 1955). A pastor's wife tells of the life of Norwegian immigrants in the Midwest in the 1850s.

Laubach, Frank. *Prayer Diary* (Westwood, N.J.: Revell, 1964). During his work in India and Africa, the famous literacy pioneer kept a record of his daily prayers.

Lee, Laurel. *Walking through the Fire: A Hospital Journal* (New York: E.P. Dutton, 1977). A young mother tells of her struggles with Hodgkin's Disease.

Livingstone, David. *Livingstone's Private Journals (1851-53),* ed. Schapera (Berkeley: Univ. of California Press, 1960). The travels and reflections of a famous missionary to Africa.

Martyn, Henry. *Selections from the Journal and Letters of Henry Martyn,* ed. Elmer H. Douglas (Nashville: The Upper Room, 1959). The spiritual insights of a missionary to India and Persia.

Merton, Thomas. *The Sign of Jonas* (New York: Doubleday, 1956). In a sequel to *The Seven Storey Mountain,* this contemporary spiritual writer tells of his life in a Trappist monastery.

Niebuhr, Reinhold. *Leaves from the Notebooks of a Tamed Cynic* (San Francisco: Harper & Row, 1980). An American theologian recounts his days as pastor of a blue-collar church in Detroit.

Nouwen, Henri J. M. *The Genessee Diary: Report from a Trappist Monastery* (Garden City, N.Y: Doubleday, 1976). A contemporary

writer shares his search for God during a seven-month stay in a
Trappist monastery.

Pope John XXIII. *Journal of a Soul,* trans. Dorothy White (New York:
McGraw-Hill, 1965). A beloved Christian leader shares the story
of his spiritual pilgrimage.

Price, Eugenia. *Diary of a Novel* (New York: Lippincott & Crowell,
1980). A Christian writer tells how she researched and wrote the
historical novel, *Margaret's Story.*

Sarton, May. *Journal of a Solitude* (New York: W. W. Norton,1973).
In this, one of her many published journals, novelist Sarton mod-
els the process of effective journal writing.

Schramm, John and Mary. *Things That Make for Peace* (Minneapolis:
Augsburg, 1976). Through journal selections and quotations
from their reading, a husband and wife share their search for a
more Christian life-style.

Simpson, Robert and Anne. *Through the Wilderness of Alzheimer's: A
Guide in Two Voices* (Minneapolis: Augsburg, 1999). A unique
book in which a husband and wife share their journals in which
they wrote their experiences as Alzheimer's patient and caregiver.

Steuck, Jeanine. *Good Morning, Judy* (Minneapolis: Augsburg, 1978).
A mother's journal, kept while her twenty-two-year-old daughter
was seriously ill.

Thielicke, Helmut. *Voyage to the Far East* (Philadelphia: Muhlenberg
Press, 1962). On a sea voyage to Southeast Asia, China, and Japan,
a German pastor and theologian captures the sights and sounds
and his thoughts on the Christian faith and Eastern religions.

_____. *African Diary: My Search for Understanding* (Waco, Tex.:
Word, 1974). On a trip to Africa, Thielicke shares his observations
on the culture, the role of the church, and the effects of missionary work.

Wesley, John. *Journal of John Wesley,* ed. Percy Livingstone Parker.
(Chicago: Moody Press, 1974). The founder of Methodism
recounts his conversion and his preaching ministry.

Whitefield, George. *Journals* (London: The Banner of Truth Trust,
1960). This early evangelical preacher tells of his inner spiritual

life and his preaching tours in America and Great Britain.

Woolman, John. *Journal of John Woolman* (New York: Corinth Books, 1961). An eighteenth-century American Quaker tells of his struggle against slavery and other social evils.

Guides to Published Journals

Brinton, Howard H. *Quaker Journals* (Wallingford, Penn.: Pendle Hill Publications, 1972). An analysis of the religious experiences described in Quaker journals and autobiographies.

Dunawy, Phillip and Mel Evans, eds. *A Treasury of the World's Great Diaries,* introduction by Louis Untermeyer. (Garden City, N.Y.: Doubleday, 1957). An excellent way to sample dozens of journals, including those of John Woolman, Mark Twain, Queen Victoria, Sir Walter Scott, Louisa May Alcott, Henry David Thoreau, and John Wesley.

Holliday, Laurel. *Heart Songs: The Intimate Diaries of Young Girls* (New York: Methuen, 1978, 1980). Don't be misled by the subtitle! This is not scandalous reading, but some excerpts from the journals of teen-age girls in Europe and America.

Lifshin, Lyn, ed. *Ariadne's Thread: A Collection of Contemporary Women's Journals* (New York: Harper & Row, 1982). A great way to sample journals by Maxine Kumin, Gail Godwin, Marge Piercy, Sylvia Plath, Anne Sexton, and others.

Mallon, Thomas. *Book of One's Own: People and Their Diaries* (New York: Penguin, 1986). A delightful discussion of journal writers under the categries of chroniclers, travelers, pilgrims, creators, apologists, confessors, and prisoners, with a bibliography of published journals.

Matthews, William. *American Diaries: An Annotated Bibliography of American Diaries Written Prior to the Year 1861* (Berkeley: Univ. of California Press, 1945). If you want to explore the world of early American diaries, here is your guide.

Ponsonby, Arthur. *English Diaries: A Review of English Diaries from the Sixteenth to the Twentieth Century* (London: Methuen, 1923), *More English Diaries: Further Reviews of Diaries from the Sixteenth to the Nineteenth Century* (London: Methuen, 1927), and *Scottish and Irish Diaries from the 16th to the 19th Century* (London: Methuen, 1927). These three volumes direct you to many historical journals written by a wide variety of writers.

Prayer and Spiritual Reading

Foster, Richard. *Prayer: Finding the Heart's True Home* (San Francisco: HarperSanFrancisco, 1992). A sound and wise book that invited us to prayer at many levels.

Foster, Richard and James Bryan Smith. *Devotional Classics: Selected Readings for Individuals and Groups* (San Francisco: HarperSanFrancisco, 1993). Fifty-two selections from a wide range of Christian writers with reflection questions and spiritual exercises.

Klug, Lyn, ed. *All Will Be Well: A Gathering of Healing Prayers* (Minneapolis: Augsburg, 1998) and *Soul Weavings: A Gathering of Women's Prayer* (Minneapolis: Augsburg, 1996). Two fine anthologies of prayers from around the world and through the ages.

Ofstedal, Paul, ed. *These Words upon Your Heart: Daily Reflections on Spiritual Classics* (Minneapolis: Augsburg, 2002). Quotations from a dozen classic spiritual writers, with reflecitons by contemporary Christians.

Owens, Barbara, ed. *Steadfast in Your Word: Daily Reflections from Martin Luther* (Minneapolis: Augsburg, 2002). A selection of spiritual passsages from the great Reformer.

Journal Writing

Adams, Kathleen. *Journal to the Self: Twenty-Two Paths to Personal Growth* (New York: Warner Books, 1990) and *The Write Way to Wellness: A Workbook for Healing and Change* (Lakewood, Col.: The Center for Journal Therapy, 2000). In these and other books and tapes, the founder of The Center for Journal Therapy shares many simple, but powerful journaling tools for healing and wholeness.

Bender, Sheila. *A Year in the Life: Journaling for Self-Discovery* (Cincinnati: Walking Stick Press, 2000) and *Keeping a Journal You Love* (Cincinnati: Walking Stick Press, 2001). These two books offer hundreds of creative ideas for expanding and deepening your journal writing.

Deer Heart, Rosalie and Alison Strickland. *Harvesting Your Journals: Writing Tools to Enhance Your Growth and Creativity* (San Cristobel, N. Mex.: Heart Link Publishers, 1999). The best book I know on how to work with your journals after they're written.

Leslie, Clare Walker and Charles E. Roth. *Keeping a Nature Journal* (Pownal, Vt.: Storey Books, 1998). A beautiful book that shows you how to "discover a whole new way of seeing the world around you."

Creative Writing

Barrington, Judith. *Writing the Memoir: From Truth to Art* (Portland, Ore.: The Eighth Mountain Press, 1997). A guide to the craft, challenges, and ethical dilemmas of writing your true stories, with many helpful writing assignments.

Fox, John. *Finding What You Didn't Lose: Expressing Your Truth and Creativity through Poem-Making* (New York: Tarcher, 1995) and *Poetic Medicine: The Healing Art of Poem-Making* (New York: Tarcher, 1997). Rich, compassionate, practical books that will liberate you to write healing poems.

Rainer, Tristine. *Your Life As Story: Writing the New Autobiography* (New York: Tarcher, 1997). The author of one of the basic books on journaling, *The New Diary*, discusses the art of turning your life experiences into story.

Notes

Chapter 1

1. Harry J. Cargas and Roger I. Radley, *Keeping a Spiritual Journal* (Garden City, N.Y.: Doubleday, 1981), p. 8.
2. *Pendle Hill Bulletin No.* 322 (October, 1981), p. 6.
3. Donald Bloesch, *The Crisis of Piety* (Grand Rapids, Mich.: Eerdmans, 1968), p. 67.
4. Richard Foster, *Celebration of Discipline* (San Francisco: Harper & Row, 1978).
5. Ibid., p. 1.
6. Ibid., p. 2.
7. Henri Nouwen, "The Desert Counsel to Flee the World," *Sojourners* (June 1980), p. 17.

Chapter 2

1. D. Martyn Lloyd-Jones, *Spiritual Depression: Its Causes and Care* (Grand Rapids, Mich.: Eerdmans, 1965), p. 15.
2. Elizabeth O'Connor, *Letters to Scattered Pilgrims* (San Francisco: Harper & Row, 1979), p. 47.
3. Frederick and Mary Ann Brussat, *Spiritual Rx* (New York: Hyperion, 2000), p. 2.
4. Richard Foster, *Freedom of Simplicity* (San Francisco: Harper & Row, 1981), p. 109.
5. R. V. Cassill, *Writing Fiction* (New York: Pocket Books, 1962), p. xv.
6. Philip Dunaway and Mel Evans, eds., *A Treasury of the World's Great Diaries* (Garden City, N. Y.: Doubleday, 1957), p. 503.
7. O'Connor, *Letters to Scattered Pilgrims*, pp. 55-56.
8. Arthur Gordon, *A Touch of Wonder* (Old Tappan, N.J.: Revell,

1974), p. 165.

9. Quoted in *Worship,* vol. 7, no. 8, p. 478.

10. Ruth Vaughn, *Write to Discover Yourself* (Garden City, N.Y.: Doubleday, 1980), pp. 5-6.

11. Elton Trueblood, *While It Is Day* (New York: Harper & Row, 1974), p. 64.

12. Douglas J. Rumford, "Keeping a Personal Journal," *Leadership* (Winter, 1981), p. 57.

13. Ibid., p. 56.

Chapter 3

1. Peter Elbow, *Writing without Teachers* (New York: Oxford Univ. Press, 1973). *Writing with Power: Techniques for Mastering the Writing Process* (New York: Oxford Univ. Press, 1981).

Chapter 4

1. Janice T. Dixon and Dora D. Flack, *Preserving Your Past* (Garden City, N.Y.: Doubleday, 1977), p. 19.

2. Percy Livingstone Parker, ed., *The Journal of John Wesley* (Chicago: Moody Press, 1974), p. 139.

3. John and Mary Schramm, *Things That Make for Peace* (Minneapolis: Augsburg, 1976), pp. 97-98. Used by permission.

4. Trueblood, *While It Is Day,* p. 24.

5. Parker, *Journal of Wesley,* p. 31.

6. Ernest Dimnet, *The Art of Thinking* (New York: Fawcett World Library, 1978), p. 159.

7. Helmut Thielicke, *Voyage to the Far East* (Philadelphia: Muhlenberg Press, 1962), p. x.

Chapter 6

1. Elizabeth O'Connor, *Eighth Day of Creation* (Waco, Tex.: Word, 1971), p. 12.

Chapter 7

1. Paul Tournier, *Adventure of Living* (New York: Harper & Row, 1976), p. 217.
2. Dietrich Bonhoeffer, *The Way to Freedom* (New York: Harper & Row, 1966), p. 59.
3. Andrew Murray, *The Inner Chamber and the Inner Life* (Grand Rapids, Mich.: Zondervan, 1950), p. 72.
4. C. S. Lewis, ed., *George Macdonald: An Anthology* (London: Geoffrey Bles: The Centenary Press, 1946), p. 23.
5. W. Tozer, *Pursuit of God* (Harrisburg, Penn.: Christian Publications, 1948), p. 81.
6. *God in the Dock: Essays on Theology and Ethics* (Grand Rapids, Mich.: Eerdmans, 1970), p. 202.
7. Avery Brooke, *Learning and Teaching Christian Meditation* (Cambridge, Mass.: Cowley, 1990), p. 15.
8. Lance Webb, *Disciplines for Life in the Age of Aquarius* (Waco, Tex.: Word, 1972), p. 12.
9. Charles F. Whiston, *Instructions in the Life of Prayer* (Cincinnati: Forward Movement Publications, 1945), p. 21.
10. C. S. Lewis, *Letters to Malcolm: Chiefly about Prayer* (New York: Harcourt, Brace and World, 1963), p. 82.

Chapter 8

1. Mark Scannell, *The Intensive Journal: Tapping the Creative Energy Within* (Minneapolis: Sycamore, 1981), p. 2.
2. These questions based in part on Dixon and Flack, *Preserving Your Past.*
3. James C. Fenhagen, *More Than Wanderers* (New York: Seabury, 1979), p.49.

Chapter 9

1. Maxwell Maltz, *Psycho-cybernetics* (Englewood Cliffs, N.J.: Prentice-Hall, 1960), pp. 57-58.
2. M. Basil Pennington, *Daily We Touch Him* (New York: Doubleday, 1977), p. 153.

Chapter 10
1. Nouwen, "Desert Counsel," p. 16
2. Parker, *Journal of Wesley,* p. 7.
3. Rumford, "Personal Journal," p. 57.

Chapter 11
1. James W. Pennebaker, *Opening Up: The Healing Power of Expressing Emotions* (New York: The Guilford Press, 1997), p. 185.
2. James W. Pennebaker, "Writing Your Wrongs," *American Health* (Jan/Feb 1991), p. 67.
3. Ibid.
4. Joshua M. Smyth, et al., "Effects of Writing about Stressful Experiences on Symptom Reduction in Patients with Asthma or Rheumatoid Arthritis," *Journal of the American Medical Association,* vol. 281, no. 14 (April 14, 1999), pp. 1304-1309.
5. "Writing as a Means of Healing; Studies Show Benefits," in *HealthFacts,* vol. 16, no. 145 (June 1991), p. 1.
6. Ibid., p. 2.
7. Louise DeSalvo, *Writing as a Way of Healing* (Boston: Beacon Press, 1999), p. 93.
8. Pennebaker, *Opening Up,* p. 24.
9. DeSalvo, p. 57.
10. S. P. Spera, et al., "Expressive Writing and Coping with Job Loss," *Academy of Management Journal,* vol. 37 (1994), pp. 722-33.

Chapter 12
1. Dunaway and Evans, *Great Diaries,* p. v.
2. Rumford, "Personal Journal," p. 57.
3. Lowell Erdahl, *Authentic Living* (New York: Abingdon, 1979), p. 39.

Chapter 13
1. Thomas Merton, *Sign of Jonas* (Garden City, N.Y.: Doubleday, 1956), p. 201.
2. O'Connor, *Scattered Pilgrims,* p. 34.

OTHER RESOURCES FROM AUGSBURG

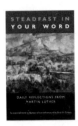

Steadfast in Your Word edited by Barbara Owen
144 pages, 0-8066-4422-2

This devotional volume of daily reflections from Martin Luther samples many sources written at various times during Luther's busy life. The themes include vocation, God's word, prayer, faith, good works, music, and the church.

These Words upon Your Heart edited by Paul Ofstedal
144 pages, 0-8066-4421-4

Quotations from the writings of classic spiritual writers provide the starting point for the devotions included in this book. Each of the contributors has written devotions based on one classic author.

All Will Be Well: A Gathering of Healing Prayers
edited by Lyn Klug
176 pages, 0-8066-3729-3

A wonderful collection of prayers that provides words and images that open a healing path. This gathering of prayers will help many speak the words of their hearts as they pray for healing in their own and others' lives.

Soul Weavings edited by Lyn Klug
160 pages, 0-8066-2849-9

A collection of rich, strong prayers that reflect the needs and experiences of women of all ages. The prayers are gathered from historic and contemporary women of faith from around the world.

Available wherever books are sold.
To order these books directly, contact:
1-800-328-4648 • www.augsburgfortress.org
Augsburg Fortress, Publishers
P.O. Box 1209, Minneapolis, MN 55440-1209